Education Studies
Reflective Reader

Education Studies
Reflective Reader

WILL CURTIS
and
ALICE PETTIGREW

LearningMatters

First published in 2010 by Learning Matters Ltd

British Library Cataloguing in Publication Data
A CIP record for this book is available from the British Library

ISBN 978 1 84445 472 3

Cover design by Topics – The Creative Partnership
Project Management by Deer Park Productions, Tavistock
Typeset by Pantek Arts Ltd, Maidstone, Kent
Printed and bound in Great Britain by Bell & Bain Ltd, Glasgow

Learning Matters Ltd
33 Southernhay East
Exeter EX1 1NX
Tel: 01392 215560
E-mail: info@learningmatters.co.uk
www.learningmatters.co.uk

Contents

Theme one: Theorising education

Theme two: Education and social justice

Theme three: Learning in the twenty-first century

The authors

Will Curtis is Education Subject Leader and Principal Lecturer in Education Studies at De Montfort University. He leads modules in Philosophy of Education, Learners and Learning, and Radical Educations, and he supervises students at undergraduate, MA and PhD levels. He has 13 years' experience of teaching on a wide range of programmes in further and higher education and has a longstanding research interest in the relationship between learning and culture. Will is currently on the Executive Committee of the British Education Studies Association.

Alice Pettigrew is a researcher currently based at the Institute of Education, University of London. Recently she has worked as a visiting lecturer at the University of the West of England where she taught undergraduate courses in *Education and Social Justice* with a particular focus on gender theory and sexuality as well as 'ethnicity', 'race' and multi-cultural citizenship. Her research has examined the relationships between education and identity from a variety of social scientific perspectives.

Acknowledgements

Every effort has been made to trace the copyright holders and to obtain their permission for the use of copyright material. The publisher and author will gladly receive any information enabling them to rectify any error or omission in subsequent editions.

Chapter 1

Phillips, M (1998) *All Must Have Prizes*. London: Little, Brown Book Group. Reprinted with permission.

Holt, J (1990) *How Children Fail*. Harmondsworth: Penguin Books Ltd. Copyright © John Holt, 1964. Reprinted by permission of A.M. Heath & Co Ltd.

Rudduck, J (2005) *Pupil Voice is Here to Stay!* QCA Futures: Meeting the Challenge. www.qcda.gov.uk/libraryAssets/media/11478_rudduck_pupil_voice_is_here_to_stay.pdf. Reprinted with permission.

Burke, C and Grosvenor I (2003) *The School I'd Like: Children and Young People's Reflections on an Education for the 21st Century*. London: Routledge. Copyright © 2003. Reproduced by permission of Taylor and Francis Books UK.

Chapter 2

Neill, AS (1968) *A Dominie's Log: The Story of a Scottish Teacher*. London: Hogarth Press. Reprinted by permission of the Random House Group Ltd.

Whitty, G (2006) *Teacher Professionalism in a New Era*; General Teaching Council for Northern Ireland's First Annual Lecture. www.gtcni.org.uk/uploads/docs/GTCNI%20Paper.doc Copyright © G Whitty, 2006. Reprinted with permission.

Apple, M (2009) Is there a place for Education in Social Transformation, in Svi Shapiro, H (ed) *Education and Hope in Troubled Times: Socio-cultural, Political and Historical Studies in Education*. Raleigh, North Carolina, USA: Copyright © 2009 by Taylor & Francis Group LLC – Books. Reproduced with permission.

Postman, N and Weingartner, C (1971) *Teaching as a Subversive Activity*. New York: Delacorte Press. Copyright © 1969 Neil Postman and Charles Weingartner. Used by permission of Dell Publishing, a Division of Random House, Inc.

Chapter 3

Woodhead, C (2009) *A Desolation of Learning: Is this the Education our Children Deserve?* Reproduced by permission of James Croft, Pencil-Sharp Publishing.

Royal Society for the encouragement of Arts, Manufactures and Commerce (RSA) (1999) *Opening Minds: Education for 21st Century*.

www.thersa.org/__data/assets/pdf_file/0005/2885/opening-minds-education-for-the-21st-century.pdf. Reprinted with permission.

Foucault, M (1991) *Discipline and Punish: The Birth of the Prison* (tr. Sheridan, A). Harmondsworth: Penguin Social Sciences. Copyright © Alan Sheridan, 1977. Reproduced by permission of Penguin Books Ltd.

Mohl, G (2007) *Innovative Student Assessment; Deliberations on Teaching and Learning in Higher Education*. www.londonmet.ac.uk/deliberations/assessment/mowl.cfm. Copyright © London Metropolitan University Editorial Board. Reprinted with permission.

Chapter 4

Bartlett, S and Burton, D (2006) Practitioner Research or Descriptions of Classroom Practice? A Discussion of Teachers Investigating their Classrooms. *Educational Action Research*, 14(3). www.tandf.co.uk/journals/titles/09650792.asp. Reproduced with permission of Taylor & Francis Group.

Punch, K (2009) *An Introduction to Research Methods in Education*. London: Sage Publications. Reproduced by permission of SAGE Publications, London, Los Angeles, New Delhi and Singapore.

Chapter 5

Brown, G (2008) *Speech to Specialist School and Academies Trust* www.number10.gov.uk/page18045. Copyright ©HMSO. Reproduced under the terms of the Crown Copyright PSI License C2010000141.

Tomlinson, S (2005) *Education in a Post-Welfare Society (2nd edition)*. Buckingham: Open University Press. Copyright © 2001. Reproduced with the kind permission of Open University Press. All rights reserved.

Ball, S (2006) *Education Policy and Social Class: The Selected Works of Stephen J. Ball*. London: Routledge. Copyright © 2006. Reproduced by permission of Taylor and Francis Books UK.

Chapter 6

Bern SL (1993) *The Lenses of Gender: Transforming the Debate of Sexual Inequality*. New Haven, Connecticut, USA: Yale University Press. Copyright © 1993. Reprinted with permission.

Department for Children, Schools and Families – DCSF (2009) *Gender and Education: Mythbusters*. http://publications.teachernet.gov.uk/eOrderingDownload/00599-2009BKT-EN.pdf. Copyright ©HMSO. Reproduced under the terms of the Crown Copyright PSI License C2010000141.

Warrington, M and Younger, M (2000) The Other Side of the Gender Gap. *Gender and Education*, 12 (4). www.tandf.co.uk/journals/titles/09540253.asp. Reproduced with permission of Taylor & Francis Group.

Chapter 7

Richardson, R and Wood, A (2000) *Inclusive Schools, Inclusive Society*. Stoke on Trent: Trentham Books Ltd. Reprinted with permission.

Gillborn, D (2008) *Racism and Education: Coincidence or Conspiracy?* London: Routledge. Copyright © 2008 Reproduced by permission of Taylor and Francis Books UK.

Jasper, L and Sewell, T (2003) *Look Beyond the Street*. www.guardian.co.uk/world/2003/jul/19/race.raceineducation.
Copyright © Lee Jasper and Tony Sewell 2003. Reprinted with permission.

Chapter 8

Mortimore, T (2008) Social and Educational Inclusion, in Ward, S (ed) *A Student's Guide to Education Studies (2nd edition)*. London: Routledge. Copyright © 2008. Reproduced by permission of Taylor and Francis Books UK.

Warnock, M (2005) *Special Educational Needs: A New Look*. London: Philosophy of Education Society of Great Britain (PESGB).
Copyright © 2005 Mary Warnock. Reprinted with permission.

Waterfield, J, West, R and Parker, M (2006) Supporting Inclusive Practice: Developing an Assessment Toolkit, in Adams, M and Brown, S (eds) *Towards Inclusive Learning in Higher Education: Developing Curricula for Disabled Students*. London: Routledge. Copyright © 2006. Reproduced by permission of Taylor and Francis Books UK.

Chapter 9

Burbules, N and Torres, C (2000) Globalization and Education: An Introduction, in Burbules, N and Torres, C (Eds) *Globalization and Education: Critical Perspectives*. New York: Routledge. Copyright © 2000. Reproduced by permission of Taylor and Francis Books USA.

Spring, J (2008) *Globalization of Education: An Introduction*. New York: Routledge. Copyright © 2008. Reproduced by permission of Taylor and Francis Books USA.

Triandis, H (2001) Individualism and Collectivism: Past, Present and Future, in Matsumoto, D *The Handbook of Culture and Psychology* New York: Oxford University Press. Reprinted with permission.

Burford, G, Ngila, L and Rafiki, Y (2003) Education, Indigenous Knowledge and Globalisation, in *Science in Africa*, 2003 (03).
www.scienceinafrica.co.za/2003/march/ik.htm. Reprinted with permission.

Chapter 10

Livingstone, S (2009) *Children and the Internet*. Cambridge: Polity. Reprinted with permission.

Cox, M, Webb, M, Abbott, C, Blakeley, B, Beauchamp, T and Rhodes V, 2003, *ICT and Pedagogy: A Review of the Research Literature*. http://publications.becta.org.uk/display.cfm?resID=25813. Reprinted with permission.

Crook, C (2008) What are Web 2.0 Technologies, and why do they Matter? in Selwyn, N (ed) *Education 2.0? Designing the Web for Teaching and Learning: A Commentary by the Technology Enhanced Learning phase of the Teaching and Learning Research Programme*. www.tlrp.org/pub/documents/TELcomm.pdf. Reprinted with permission.

Selwyn, N (2008) Learning and Social Networking, in Selwyn, N (ed) *Education 2.0? Designing the Web for Teaching and Learning: A Commentary by the Technology Enhanced Learning phase of the Teaching and Learning Research Programme* www.tlrp.org/pub/documents/TELcomm.pdf. Reprinted with permission.

Chapter 11

Smith, M (1997) *A Brief History of Thinking About Informal Education*. London: Infed. www.infed.org/thinkers/et-hist.htm. Reproduced with permission from the Encyclopaedia of Informal Education.

Illich, I (2000) *Deschooling Society*. London: Marion Boyars. Reprinted with permission.

Facer, K (2009) *Educational, Social and technological futures: a report from the Beyond Current Horizons programme*. Bristol: Futurelab. Reprinted with permission from Futurelab under Creative Commons License. Copyright © HMSO. Reproduced under the terms of the Crown Copyright PSI License C2010000141.

Introduction

The *Quality Assurance Agency for Higher Education Studies* suggest that, as a student of Education Studies, you should be able to:

• draw from a range of sources, perspectives and disciplines;

• engage with fundamental questions about the aims and values of education;

• interrogate educational processes in various contexts; and

• develop qualities of independence and critical engagement.

(QAA, 2007)

It is with these principles in mind that we have written the *Education Studies Reflective Reader* which brings together edited extracts from seminal works, recent policy documents, empirical research, web-based exchanges and contemporary literature. We have tried to select readings that might be considered provocative and that should stimulate and engage you: many of the extracts offer fresh and innovative ways of thinking about taken-for-granted aspects of education and 'common sense' assumptions about what goes on inside universities and schools. We hope that they will encourage you to reflect critically on key issues of relevance to the study of education today.

In each chapter, the readings form the stimulus for discussion. We set the context for each extract, providing an introductory overview of related themes, arguments and ideas. Competing or contradictory perspectives are provided, as well as further critical analysis. The chapters include clear learning outcomes and summaries as well as details of suggested further reading and useful websites. Points to Consider boxes follow each extract to help structure your thinking around the issues raised. Occasional Scenario boxes help you to reflect on the practical implications of the literature.

The book is organised around three themes. The first theme – *Theorising education* – introduces you to some of the main dimensions of education – the learner, teacher, curriculum and assessment – and considers the processes involved in educational research. Chapter 1 asks what it means to be a learner in the twenty-first century, encouraging you to reflect on the aspects of schooling that impact positively and negatively on learning experience. It looks in particular detail at notions of learner voice, and discusses effective strategies for enabling learners to participate in the development and evaluation of their educational experiences. Chapter 2 looks at the role of the teacher. It points to changes in the meaning of teacher professionalism as the educational environment becomes increasingly dominated by markets and standards. Extracts from 'radical' educators encourage you to challenge assumptions about the role of the teacher (and what it means to teach). Chapter 3 focuses on two centrally important educational concepts – curriculum and assessment. It asks you to reflect on the dominance of subject-centred curricular and assessment via examination in schools, colleges and universities today. Alternatives to both are outlined and discussed. Chapter 4 concludes the section by examining the relationship between educational practice, education policy and educational research. It considers the position of teachers and students within the research process and describes differences between positivist and intrepretative approaches to data collection and analysis.

The second theme – *Education and social justice* – is concerned with social identities, social inequalities and the roles that formal systems of education can play in reproducing and/ or challenging these. Chapter 5 emphasises the political significance of education – both at the level of national government and in terms of the personal decisions that individuals make – by considering relationships between education, social mobility and socio-economic class. Chapter 6 includes an extract drawn from the wider field of gender theory and suggests that such theoretical understandings can be valuable if we want to critically examine apparent differences in the educational experiences of males and females. Chapter 7 considers the significance of 'race' and 'ethnicity' within education. The extracts investigate the charge that Britain's schools are 'institutionally racist'. Chapter 8 examines key debates and issues related to special educational needs, identifying and discussing the wide range of learning 'difficulties' and 'differences' that are covered by the term. It considers the benefits and difficulties related to the integration of children with special educational needs into mainstream schools, encouraging you to reflect on the role of specialist institutions. It considers the current emphasis on inclusion – the extent that educational structures can be adapted to meet the diverse needs of all learners.

The third theme – titled *Learning in the twenty-first century* – looks at three of the most prominent issues for education at present and in the near future. Chapter 9 describes and discusses the complex set of processes commonly characterised as 'globalisation' and considers implications for education of these. Chapter 10 considers the impact of new technologies on learning and the teacher. You will be encouraged to reflect on how the internet has effected childhood and how new technologies are used in the classroom today. There is a specific focus on Web 2.0 technologies, which enable users to create, share and discuss their own online material. The final chapter considers education beyond schooling, looking at the wide array of learning experiences that take place outside formal settings. You will question how social and technological developments impact on schooling and the centrality of networks to educational futures.

There is so much interesting material to read in the study of education. This book is a starting point: we encourage you to use it as a gateway. If you find the extracts interesting, read the rest of the book or article and use the references you find there to delve a little deeper still.

REFERENCES

QAA (2007) *Subject Benchmark Statements: Education Studies*
www.qaa.ac.uk/academicinfrastructure/benchmark/honours/educationstudies.asp

Theme one
Theorising education

Chapter 1
The learner

O B J E C T I V E S

By the end of this chapter you should have:
- evaluated the claim that contemporary educational structures are harmful to learners;
- thought about strategies that support learners in becoming engaged and motivated;
- explored the characteristics of an effective learner;
- reflected upon the benefits of giving learners the opportunity to participate in conversations about their own learning;
- considered the kinds of structures, cultures and relationships that provide for the most positive learner voice encounters.

Introduction

It goes without saying – educational institutions exist for the sake of learners. Most learners have heard an exasperated teacher claiming something like, *I'm not the one who needs to be here!* or *You're only wasting your own time*. While we might argue about who should learn, and what, where and how they should learn it, we can agree that a school's raison d'etre is its learners. And yet, for much of the history of formal schooling, the experiences and interests of learners seem to have been rather secondary. Greater attention has been paid to other factors: to the subjects that make up the curriculum, to preparation and training for the workplace, and to the cultivation of qualities like obedience, discipline and conformity. Educational 'experts' had the responsibility for devising and evaluating these educational structures. Although Rousseau was arguing for learner-centred education as far back as 1762, it is only recently that the perspectives of children and young people have been systematically gathered as a means of informing policy and practice.

As such, it is a fascinating time to reflect on the experiences of learners today. We have written elsewhere on the subject of learners and learning in the contemporary world (Curtis and Pettigrew, 2009). Recent transformations in the culture and structure of society are impacting on the attitudes, skills and requisite needs of learners in the twenty-first century: the unprecedented pace and scope of change; developments in information and communication technologies (most notably, the internet, email, mobile technologies and mass media); globalisation and the increasing mobility of people; commodities and ideas; and the democratisation, fragmentation, diversification, fluidity and unpredictability of contemporary life. We return to many of these issues in the third theme of this book.

The first chapter reflects on how certain features of education might impact negatively on learners. Then it discusses the types of environments that are most likely to promote engaging learning experiences, exploring the means by which young people can most effectively learn. It focuses on learner voice in particular: on why providing learners with the opportunity to participate in the creation and evaluation of their own learning can be beneficial – for learners as well as for teachers, schools and policy makers. The chapter concludes by considering the ideas that are generated when learners are given a voice.

Is schooling beneficial for learners?

The first two extracts offer criticisms of the impact of formal schooling on learners. While the accounts come from very different perspectives, they are both illustrative of a key difficulty for educational systems – how can the multitude of experiences, interests, needs and skills of all learners be accommodated? For Phillips, educational policy-makers' response has been to reduce expectations and standards to the lowest common denominator, thereby harming the interests of all. For Holt, the response has been to construct institutions that reclassify learning as the passive absorption of information and the accumulation of certificates, resulting in learners who have lost interest in the process of learning itself.

EXTRACT ONE

Phillips, M (1998) All Must Have Prizes. *London: Little Brown, pages 12–13*

Here in a nutshell is one of the driving impulses behind the thinking that has caused educational standards across the board to implode. At some point in the last few decades, the educational world came to agree that its overriding priority was to make children feel good about themselves: none of them should feel inferior to anyone else or a failure. At the same time, such people came to believe that children from relatively impoverished backgrounds who unarguably started at a clear disadvantage, were somehow incapable of learning what other, more forward, children could learn. There was, of course, not a shred of evidence for such a belief. What disadvantaged children needed above all was more structured teaching, greater attention paid to those elementary rules of language or of arithmetic and a heavier emphasis on order. These were all features which were second nature to those children from more favoured homes but which tended to be lacking in their own.

But the educational world, heavily influenced by other profound currents of thinking which all conspired to undermine every form of external authority (and which are examined in more detail later), decided in its wisdom that disadvantaged children simply couldn't learn those 'difficult' things. Moreover, since it now held that no child was allowed to be better than any other, it decided that no child would learn them. Thus was created an examination system – the GCSE – which was structured so that many more children would be able to pass it. The only way the education establishment could attempt to square the circle it had set itself was by lowering the standard. And the teaching of individual subjects was similarly refined in such a way that it appeared no child could fail to cope with them. So no rules of language, for example, were to be taught: after all, if no rules were taught, no child could fail to learn them. Nothing was to be difficult; everything in the education garden was to be fun. The uncomfortable truth that little of value is achieved without effort, in education as elsewhere, was decried as a form of child abuse.

But circles, of course, cannot be squared and the attempt was accordingly misguided. It claimed to elevate equality to the highest virtue. But what it actually imposed, through the most doctrinaire means possible, was an equality of ignorance and under-achievement. It meant not only that every child was to be equally uneducated, not only that the brightest were stripped both of knowledge and of those challenges that would stretch them, but that the most disadvantaged children, those very children for whose benefit this was all ostensibly conceived, were left worst off of all – effectively abandoned and trapped in disadvantage by their grievous lack of a proper education. It was, indeed, a liberal ideal that was now in the process of destroying itself.

POINTS TO CONSIDER

- *Phillips is highly critical of a perceived intent for everything in the education garden to be fun.*

  - *How far does this characterise your experience of formal schooling?*

  - *What are the advantages and disadvantages of fun as a cornerstone of educational experience?*

- *Do you think the UK has a no fail educational system?*

  - *Why might it be preferable for schools to produce a certain proportion of learners who fail?*

  - *Why might it be preferable for everyone who completes compulsory schooling to achieve?*

- *What evidence can you find that suggests educational standards have lowered in recent years? Can you find evidence to the contrary?*

- *What do you think Phillips means by a proper education?*

- *What kinds of curriculum and schooling structures and/or classroom strategies might be employed so that the needs of advantaged and disadvantaged learners might be more effectively met?*

So, is it difficult to fail in the UK education system today? Around 30,000 children (5 per cent of pupils) each year leave school without any qualifications (Tickle, 2006). Many of these leave school long before they reach the age of 16, with sizeable numbers of permanent exclusion from compulsory schooling. The UK compares unflatteringly with other European countries in terms of the number of 16–24 year-olds categorised as NEET – not in education, employment or training – with just under one million in March 2010. As such, large numbers of young people are leaving schooling disaffected and disengaged.

Given that young people are required to study for at least eleven years of their lives, shouldn't they all receive a *prize* for what they have achieved? What a terrible waste of time if they leave school without any qualifications. Moreover, evidence suggests that educational failure is a powerful indicator of anti-social and criminal activity in later life. The problem with education might not be that *all must have prizes*, rather that *too many get no prizes* – and that exclusion from these educational prizes not only impacts negatively on the individuals who fail, but also on society as a whole.

Fear of failure

John Holt, an influential American advocate of homeschooling, offers us a very different take from Phillips on schooling and failure. Writing prior to the policy interventions that Phillips is critical of, Holt argues that schools teach children to fear failure, to suppress their innate curiosity and to become dependent on external rewards as motivation to learn. In the following extract, Holt talks about his seventeen-month-old niece and the qualities she possesses as a learner. While the first section is written in 1960, the indented later section is written in 1983 – where he reflects on changes since he first wrote the book.

EXTRACT TWO

Holt, J (1990) How Children Fail. *Harmondsworth: Penguin Books, pages 111–113*

July 20, 1960

My seventeen-month-old niece caught sight of my ball-point pen the other day, and reached out for it. It has a plastic cap that fits over the point. She took hold of it, and after some pushing and pulling, got the cap off. After looking it over, she put it back on. Then off again; then on again. A good game! Now, if I want to be able to use my pen, I have to keep it out of sight, for when she sees it, she wants to play with it. She is so deft in putting it back on that it makes me wonder about all I've read about the lack of coordination in infants and the imprecision of their movements. Under the right circumstances – when they are interested – they may be more skilful than we think.

These quiet summer days I spend many hours watching this baby. What comes across most vividly is that she is a kind of scientist. She is always observing and experimenting. She is hardly ever idle. Most of her waking time she is intensely and purposefully active, soaking up experience and trying to make sense out of it, trying to find how things around her behave, and trying to make them behave as she wants them to.

In the face of what looks like unbroken failure, she is so persistent. Most of her experiments, her efforts to predict and control her environment, don't work. But she goes right on, not the least daunted. Perhaps this is because there are no penalties attached to failure, except nature's – usually, if you try to step on a ball, you fall down. A baby does not react to failure as an adult does, or even a five-year-old, because she has not yet been made to feel that failure is shame, disgrace, a crime. Unlike her elders, she is not concerned with protecting herself against everything that is not easy and familiar; she reaches out to experience, she embraces life.

Watching this baby, it is hard to credit the popular notion that without outside rewards and penalties children will not learn. There are some rewards and penalties in her life; the adults approve of some things she does, and disapprove of others. But most of the time she lives beyond praise or blame, if only because most of her learning experiments are unobserved. After all, who thinks about the meaning of what a baby is doing, so long as she is quiet and contented? But watch a while and think about it, and you see that she has a strong desire to make sense of the world around her. Her learning gives her great satisfaction, whether anyone else notices it or not.

This idea that children won't learn without outside rewards and penalties, or in the debased jargon of the behaviourists, 'positive and negative reinforcements,' usually becomes a self-fulfilling prophecy. If we treat children long enough as if that were true, they will come to believe it is true. So many people have said to me, 'If we didn't make children do things, they wouldn't do anything.' Even worse, they say, 'If I weren't made to do things, I wouldn't do anything.'

It is the creed of a slave.

When people say that terrible thing about themselves, I say, 'You may believe that, but I don't believe it. You didn't feel that way about yourself when you were little. Who taught you to feel that way?' To a large degree, it was school. Do the schools teach this message by accident, or on purpose? I don't know, and I don't think they know. They teach it because, believing it, they can't help acting as if it were true.

POINTS TO CONSIDER

- *How convincing do you find Holt's claim that children are born learners – with a natural fearlessness of failure and a joy in the processes of problem solving and experimentation? What evidence can you find to support or refute such claims?*

- *What features of schooling might have the impact of turning children against this innate love of learning?*

- *Would you learn without potential rewards or punishments – for instance, if your work would not be assessed, or if there were no grading systems at the end of your course?*

- *What classroom ethos would promote the kind of learning that Holt describes? How might this be created?*

Holt's ideas remain popular, with many claiming they have more pertinence today than when he wrote them (see Harber, 2009). In particular, Holt and others help us to question the extent that the purpose of schooling is to motivate us and to teach us how to learn. Rather, from this perspective, the experience of schooling inhibits natural inquisitiveness in the learner and promotes an instrumental outlook (that prioritises grades and other measurable achievements) in its place. A school system that emphasises transmission of knowledge and assessment has the effect of fostering and rewarding qualities like passivity and conformity. These take away from the joy of learning, making the learner study for external rewards instead of learning for its own sake.

Engaging learning experiences

Both Phillips and Holt offer critiques of formal schooling and the negative impact it has on the learner. But the vast majority of people view schooling far more positively. Throughout the twentieth and twenty-first centuries, many educational theorists and practitioners have placed the learner at the heart of their work, attempting to develop more effective ways of engaging learners. The idea that education is learner-centred rather than subject-centred has gained greater currency of late. Constructivist theories, which conceive of learners as the co-author of knowledge, meaning, learning environments and their own identities, have become increasingly prominent. A heightened interest in, and understanding of, the experiences of learners is increasingly popularising more participatory and democratic classroom practices. As Gordon, discussing the implementation of constructivist theories, states:

> *Teaching should promote experiences that require students to become active, scholarly participators in the learning process. Windshitl (1999) goes on to note that 'such experiences include problem-based learning, inquiry activities, dialogues with peers and teachers that encourage making sense of the subject matter, exposure to multiple sources of information, and opportunities for students to demonstrate their understanding in diverse ways'.*

(Gordon, 2009, page 39)

SCENARIO

Recently, significant attention has been paid to the cultivation of meta-cognitive skills in learners: the process whereby an individual develops the capacity to reflect and act upon her or his own learning – often referred to as knowing about knowing, thinking about thinking *or* learning about learning. *Three of the more well-known strategies at present are:*

- *assessment for learning;*
- *accelerated cognition;*
- *learning to learn.*

There are website links with information about each at the end of the chapter.

Guy Claxton is one of the chief proponents of the third of these – learning to learn. This means acquiring the following dispositions:

- changing and learning – *a sense that I can change and continue to learn;*
- critical curiosity – *getting below the surface, asking questions;*
- meaning making – *making a bigger picture by fitting information together;*

- creativity – *finding new ways to approach information and situations;*

- resilience – *being able to resist distractions from inside and outside and to tolerate the feelings of learning;*

- strategic awareness – *planning, resourcing and using learning preferences to complete a task;*

- learning relationships – *being able to work alone and in collaboration.*

(Demos, 2004, page 10)

Imagine you are a teacher, charged with supporting the development of these dispositions in the learners you teach. What qualities might the culture in the classroom possess? What types of strategies and activities might you might employ in your class?

To facilitate appropriate classroom activities for their learners, do you think teachers need to learn how to learn themselves? Look again at the seven dimensions of 'learning power' above – have you learnt how to learn?

Giving learners a voice

One especially fashionable method for engaging learners in their own learning is based around the notion of voice. Variously termed pupil-, student- or learner-voice, this includes a number of strategies that encourage young people to participate in the construction and evaluation of their educational experiences – to take a degree of ownership over learning, teaching and school policy. Recent years have seen a rapid expansion in the number and forms of learner consultation at all levels of education: including student councils, pupil representation on interview panels and governing boards, students as partners in pedagogic research, and a variety of other formal and informal staff-student consultative arrangements. In the following extract, Jean Rudduck offers some of the main arguments in favour of *pupil voice*.

Rudduck, J (2003) Pupil voice is here to stay! QCA Futures: Meeting the Challenge

Recent years have seen a wealth of statements supporting the idea of young people in school finding and using their voices:

'The fact is that pupils themselves have a huge potential contribution to make, not as passive objects but as active players in the education system.' [i]

'Students can and should participate, not only in the construction of their own learning environments, but as research partners in examining questions of learning and anything else that happens in and around schools.' [ii]

Why has 'pupil voice' gained such a high profile? Will it turn out to be just another quick innovative buzz or is there the potential to build a new order of experience for young people in schools?

What do we mean by pupil voice?

Pupil voice is the consultative wing of pupil participation. Consultation is about talking with pupils about things that matter in school. It may involve: conversations about teaching and learning; seeking advice from pupils about new initiatives; inviting comment on ways of solving problems that are affecting the teacher's right to teach and the pupil's right to learn; inviting evaluative comment on recent developments in school or classroom policy and practice.

Arguments in support of pupil voice

These four are heard most often and are perhaps the most persuasive:

Argument 1: We need a better fit between young people's capabilities and their standing and responsibility in school; talking to pupils can help us bridge the gap

We need a more accomplished way of recognising and harnessing young people's capabilities and insights. Pupils have a lot to tell us about ways of strengthening their commitment to learning in school; they say they want:

- *to be treated in more adult ways and to have more responsibility*

- *to have choices and make decisions*

- *more opportunities to talk about what helps and what hinders their learning.*

Argument 2: The Children's Rights movement is behind it and 'everybody's doing it!'

The United Nations Convention on the Rights of the Child and the subsequent Children's Act highlight the importance of young people having their say on matters that concern them, both in and out of school. Ofsted inspection frameworks for pupil participation and consultation offer a useful set of benchmarks for monitoring the development of pupil voice.

Many national and local agencies and professional groups have an interest in pupil voice. It is one of the nine gateways to personalised learning and it is also fundamental to the realisation of citizenship education in the community of the school.

Argument 3: School improvement gains from pupil participation

An American researcher sets the scene:

'Decades of calls for educational reform have not succeeded in making schools places where all young people want to and are able to learn. It is time to invite pupils to join the conversations about how we might accomplish that.' [iii]

Among the pragmatic arguments from a Canadian policy maker iv, the strongest is the appeal to students as experts in the task of improving their experiences of learning in school; these are some of his other arguments:

- *students' views can help mobilise staff and parent opinion in favour of meaningful reform*

- *constructivist learning, which is increasingly important to high standards reforms, requires a more active student role in school*

- *students are the producers of school outcomes, so their involvement is fundamental to all improvement.*

Argument 4: The qualities that we look for in young people are those that participation and consultation can help develop...

The table identifies four generalised 'pupil states' whose reality teachers readily recognise:

	PASSIVE		
	Accepting	**Indifferent**	
	• attends regular	• mistrust of school and teachers	
	• quite likes school and teachers	• withdraws from sources of support	
	• does what is required	• denies concern about progress	
	• trusts school to deliver a future	• does not look ahead	
POSITIVE			**NEGATIVE**
	• wants to understand and contribute	• is skilled at disrupting teaching and learning	
	• wants to discuss progress in learning	• behaviour is anti-social	
	• is ready to organise things and take responsibility	• attends irregularly	
	• is ready to help other pupils	• frequently on report and sometimes excluded	
	Influencing	**Rejecting**	
	ACTIVE		

The 'positive-passive' pupil may be more compliant and easier to teach but with the new emphasis on the school as a community, teachers are increasingly valuing the 'positive-active' pupil. And looking to life beyond school, employers seem to be valuing similar qualities: a capacity for independent initiative, working collaboratively, and competence in the management of time and task. Consultation can help develop these qualities.

> **EXTRACT THREE** *continued*
>
> i   Hodgkin, R, Partnership with pupils, *Children UK, Summer 1998*
>
> ii Edwards, J. and Hattam, R, Using students as researchers in educational research: beyond silenced voices, *unpublished discussion paper for the Students Completing Schooling Project, US, 2000*
>
> iii Cook-Sather, A, Authorising students' perspectives: toward trust, dialogue, and change in education, *Educational Researcher, 2002, 31,4, pages 3–14*
>
> iv Levin, B, Putting students at the centre in education reform, *unpublished paper, Canada, 1999*
>
> v   Nixon, J, Martin, J, McKeown, PO and Ranson, S, Encouraging learning, *Open University Press, Buckingham, 1996*

> **POINTS TO CONSIDER**
>
> - *Why might learner voice have the potential to build a new order of experience for young people in schools?*
>
> - *What strategies might you employ to enable learners to participate:*
>
>   - *In the construction of their learning environments?*
>
>   - *As partners in research about learning and teaching?*
>
> - *Why might strategies like this encourage young people to want to go to school?*
>
> - *Reflect on your own experiences of school, college and university. In what ways were you given a voice? Did this impact positively on your experiences as a learner? Why?*

Assessing voice strategies

The effectiveness of strategies that advance the voices of learners varies considerably. This depends on factors such as the capacity for learners to express their opinions appropriately, the extent that these voices are representative of the entire learner cohort, and the degree to which these voices are heard and acted upon. Rudduck and Fielding (2006) identify three *big issues* that dictate how successful student voice strategies are:

- *power relations between teachers and students* – developing a partnership of open, trusting dialogue between learners and teachers;

- *a commitment to authenticity* – that teachers convey genuine interest in what learners have to say and that, where appropriate, student viewpoints influence practice;

- the *principle of inclusiveness* – allowing a diversity of voices and opinions to be heard, rather than depending on the most vocal, articulate and socially confident members of the student cohort.

Like other strategies for engaging learners, student voice is at its most effective as an essential and embedded characteristic of whole-school culture: where the school ethos places consultation and partnership between learners and staff at the very centre, where a wide range of strategies take place so that learner-staff dialogue becomes a normalised and valued part of the institutional routine. Conversely, isolated practices and events risk being viewed as half-hearted, cosmetic and superficial – *a tokenistic nod in the direction of consumerism* (Rudduck and Fielding, 2006, page 229), rather than a genuine and sustained attempt to foster democratic dialogue and collaboration between all members of an institution.

Correspondingly, perhaps the most significant learner-voice practices are not the modest victories of the school council. Rather they are the daily opportunities for learners to engage in exploratory classroom-based collaborative conversations with one another. During such interactive activities, children and young people learn through their own shared, built-up insights. They take ownership of their own learning and, in doing so, develop lifelong voice skills – to articulate their views and ideas, to talk, listen and discuss, and to work together for the achievement of shared goals.

So what do learners say?

In 1967, The *Observer* newspaper ran a competition asking children to design the school they would like to go to. There were nearly 1000 entries and many of these were included in an influential book by Edward Blishen (1969). Using this study as inspiration, The *Guardian* newspaper hosted a similar competition in 2001. More than 1500 schools responded, with over 15,000 entries from children and young people at all stages of education. They were charged with designing the secondary school of the future. Teachers supported the project, setting homework tasks such as to write about or draw the 'ideal school'. Submissions took the form of essays, videos, models, stories, designs, pictures, poems, plays and photographs (Burke and Grosvenor, 2003 pages xi–xii). As in the 1960s, a book was published that used the children's proposals to identify themes and trends. What follows in the final extract is a sample of the contributions included in that book.

EXTRACT FOUR

Burke and Grosvenor (2003) The School I'd Like: Children and Young People's Reflections on an Education for the 21st Century. *London: Routledge, pages 73–77*

In the pretty, lively school there are lots of different classes. *There are language lessons on French and German, also there are maths and history lessons. You can go to whatever class you feel like any day. The teachers are kind and interested in the children's ideas... The most important thing is learning is fun.*

Alix, 7, Oxford

I think we could learn a lot more if we had smaller class sizes of about 20. *If you had smaller class sizes then you could have more one to one. You could also have specialist teachers in to teach us, for example in cookery if we were making cakes then we could get a person in to teach us who actually makes cakes for a living.*

Helen, 12, Gosforth

Some parents or grandparents didn't have the facilities or the technology when they were at school *which is why I think that once a week they should be able to come into school and learn about some of the new teaching methods in the curriculum with their children.*

Christie, 12, Gosforth

Learning can be thirsty work *and to keep the minds of pupils working, they would be offered refreshments to relax the student at work feeding the imagination as well as listening to music to soothe and stimulate the brain.*

Stacey, 13, Stoke Golding

My ideal school would be a fun environment to learn in. *For example in some schools, the walls, the corridors and halls are often quite drab making the pupil miserable thus affecting their grades. If there were to be bright colours on the walls, carpets, ceilings etc pupils would feel happier and more in control of what they were doing enabling their grades to rise. It probably encourage[s] pupils to learn more, much faster. Pupils would also feel happier to come to school. Lessons could be taught using games and methods for fun. This would also help the things needed to be learnt stick in the pupils' mind for longer as they would have something to remember it by!*

Nadia, 12, Chertsey

For learning instead of a blackboard there will be a 1 m 16 cm by 2 m 39 cm television. *The T.V. will be turned into sky digital and all David Attenborough video collections so we can learn about wildlife. Each pupil will have a laptop with built in security system.*

Joe, 9, Clacton-on-Sea

I want more homework.

Hannah, 4, Barnsley

[...] Trips, Let's go!
We all love trips, and we can learn so much from going and seeing things.
Numeracy hour and literacy hour can be boring. LET US OUT!
The teachers and the children would love more organised outings, but I bet the Department of Education says no. In other countries the less formal approach is very successful, so why not give it a go?

Kimberley, 11, Swanwick

[...] The place must be unafraid of kids staring out of windows *and must not insist on 100% attention or even 100% attendance... It is a terrible pressure for kids to have to pay attention and to think what they are told to think. I would encourage people to dream more and enjoy the sun and the sky, the growing grass and the bear [sic] boughed trees. I would encourage kids to look beyond the classroom, out of the classroom and see themselves doing different things.*

Hero Joy, home educated, 14, Kent

[...] Pupils will decide what they want to learn and learn it. Each pupil will work on their own projects, producing them in any way they like. They will then have something to be proud of. They will receive help from people working at the school and fellow pupils, as everyone will be seen as having valid knowledge and opinions. Books and resources will be available and pupils can go to relevant places, or meet with experts. They will not be 'taken' anywhere – they will arrange trips etc. themselves. Each project, when it is finished, will be handed in; not to be marked (after all how can someone be entitled to invade work with red ink and brand it with a letter of the alphabet?) but to teach others about what the pupil has learned.

Because everyone will be learning different things there will be no set classes. Pupils will not be expected to work with and like others just because they were all born between the same two dates. Students will be able to choose where and with whom they work.

I must admit to my share of graffiti on the science lab gas taps as sixty students have gathered (and have spent half an hour being herded) around a desk to watch water boil. If the teacher had simply recognised that we were people with brains she would have realised that we all knew what water looks like while boiling. She could have said 'When water boils...' and got on with the lesson, instead of driving me to the frustration it takes to write 'Get me out of this f***ing dump' in pencil, not even caring about the possibility of her wrath if caught. (Fortunately my comment went unnoticed amongst all the other clumsily worded cries for salvation that decorated the physics lab.)

Miriam, 15, Reading

[...] This place of learning should never be somewhere to fear, nor should it restrict free speech and ideas, or be somewhere which will strip you of the confidence and individuality you need to succeed in life. School is there to prepare you for your future life, not to make you scared of it. My ideal school is a community, which upholds your strong points and overcomes your weak points. Teachers should always know how much they should be involved in your private life, but they refrain from depriving you of a life outside school untainted by the shackles of school work.

What is education if it is not about people? If results are what the government wants, then replace every child with a robot each one the same, producing the same work, the same results year after year. Education should be working to make people valuable citizens, not so called 'valuable statistics'.

Angela, 15, Croydon

- Can you identify any commonalities/trends in these children's responses – what they don't like about their present experiences and/or what they would like to happen instead?

- Do you see anything in these quotes that supports the claims of Holt, Phillips or Rudduck?

- Consider how these children's perspectives might be utilised to inform future educational policy and practice on both micro (classroom) and macro (national policy) levels.

Most of the ideas the children share are feasible and many of them are very persuasive. They tell us what we would expect (more time outdoors and fun learning environments) and some that seem counterintuitive (more homework). All the contributions demonstrate children's capacity for imagination and creativity, offering us fresh, innovative, even radical ideas – for instance, parents and grandparents studying alongside their children, disbanding sets and year groups, voluntary attendance and long-term individual projects that are not assessed by teachers. Many current issues are evident in these few comments – schools as communities, minimising fear of schooling, making use of technology and game-based learning, making use of expertise from outside the school, creating stimulating learning environments, peer-to-peer teaching, providing more informal learning opportunities and so on.

Simply reading this small sample of viewpoints, you learn a lot about who children are today, their hopes and fears, how different they are from one another, and what they like and dislike about their learning experiences. For instance, Miriam – who we hope ends up as Secretary of State for Education – provides us with a great insight into disruptive behaviour with her graffiti in the science lab. Like many of the other accounts, it warns us of relying on an adult conception of childhood in our design for schooling and our pedagogic approaches.

C H A P T E R   S U M M A R Y

This chapter began by considering the idea that schooling might be detrimental to learners. In the first two extracts, you encountered two very different perspectives – one arguing that an apparent *no fail* education system traps children from deprived background in disadvantage, the other arguing that schooling, through the imposition of rewards and punishments, inhibits the natural curiosity and experimentalism of young learners. The chapter continued by looking at the types of educational environments that encourage learners to participate actively in their own learning, focusing especially on notions of pupil/student voice. It suggested that learner voice strategies depend on open and trusting relationships, authenticity and inclusiveness and that they are at their most effective when voice is a central component of the whole school ethos. Finally, a selection of voices from learners who took part in the *The School I'd Like* project were presented and the benefits of including learner perspectives in the construction of policy, as well as the evaluation of learning and teaching, were reflected upon.

REFERENCES

Blishen, E (ed.) (1969) *The School That I'd Like*. Harmondsworth: Penguin Books

Curtis, W and Pettigrew, A (2009) *Learning in contemporary culture*. Exeter: Learning Matters

Demos (2004) *About Learning: Report of the learning working group*. London: Demos

Gordon, M (2009) "Towards a pragmatic discourse of constructivism: reflections on lessons from practice", *Educational studies: journal of the American Educational Studies Association*, 45 (1) pp39–58

Harber, C (2009) *Toxic schooling: how schools became worse*. Nottingham: Educational Heretics Press

Rousseau, J (2007) *Emile, or on education*. Sioux Falls: NuVision Publications [first published in 1762]

Rudduck, J & Fielding, M (2006) 'Student voice and the perils of popularity' *Educational review*, 58, (2) pp219–231

Tickle, L (2006) 'You just feel: I'm a failure'. *The Guardian*, 26 August 2006

Claxton, G (2008) *What's the point of school? Rediscovering the heart of education.* Oxford: Oneworld Publications

Demos (2004) *About Learning: Report of the learning working group.* London: Demos

Rudduck, J and McIntyre, D (2007) *Improving learning by consulting pupils (Improving learning series)* London: Routledge

http://arrts.gtcni.org.uk/gtcni/handle/2428/4623 – 10 principles for Assessment of Learning

www.ssat-inet.net/default.aspx – International Networking for Educational Transformation (iNet)

www.studentvoice.co.uk/ – English Secondary Students' Association

www.cognitiveacceleration.co.uk/

www.campaign-for-learning.org.uk/cfl/index.asp

Chapter 2
The teacher

OBJECTIVES

By the end of this chapter you should have:
- interrogated assumptions about the role of the teacher as disciplinarian;
- considered the changing nature of educational professionalism;
- examined the extent that recent educational policy supports and/or undermines the capacity of the teacher to perform her duties effectively;
- identified and evaluated a range of alternative teaching practices.

Introduction

Is a good teacher born or made? What characteristics does a 'good teacher' have anyway – and are they primarily related to personal qualities, professional skills or subject proficiency? Is teaching principally concerned with transmitting knowledge in a field of expertise or with cultivating qualities such as creativity, self-confidence and independence in the young people they are charged with (albeit briefly)? Should teachers teach the world as it *is* or the world as it *could be*?

It is easy to find stories of good and bad teachers – we have all been taught by both. It is less easy to agree what makes a teacher good or bad. There is no definitive rule book – despite consecutive governments' attempts to dictate the content of the curriculum, of a 'good' lesson, appropriate teacher training provision, school priorities, expected targets and standards. In this chapter, the selected extracts encourage you to reflect on the relationship between teaching and discipline and social justice. You will question what it means to be a teaching professional today and encounter some ideas that are radically different from teaching as it presently exists.

Teaching and discipline

You do not need to look too hard at mainstream educational discourses to find evidence of a focus on discipline in schools. A perceived lack of classroom discipline is frequently associated with wider anti-social behaviour among younger age groups. Many blame teachers for lacking the skills to maintain control of their classrooms. Others argue that the current educational climate inhibits the capacity for teachers to discipline: a lack of corporal punishment and other tough deterrents, an increasingly litigious society making teachers fearful of imposing strict restraints, or a perceived imbalance between the rights of the pupil and the authority of the teacher.

To address this issue the government appointed a 'behaviour tsar', with the task of reporting on progress in tackling poor school discipline. Sir Alan Steer, who recently claimed that schools too easily exclude disruptive children and should instead give them a *right royal rollicking* (Wardrop, 2009), completed his report in April 2009 (Steer, 2009). Among other things, he argues that teachers need to be made more aware of their rights, be trained more effectively in behaviour management and that improving behaviour is the responsibility of government, schools, teachers, parents and pupils in partnership (Steer, 2009, page 7). In response, the government collaborated with the NASUWT union to produce a leaflet *School Discipline: Your Powers and Rights as a Teacher* (DCSF, 2009), which outlines teachers' legal powers and rights to discipline pupils.

Popular and policy discourses appear to place discipline right at the heart of education today. But this assumption raises some important questions. Should we presuppose that the role of the teacher is to discipline the children she teaches? And, if so, what do we mean by 'discipline' and how should we go about teaching (or enforcing) it? In the first extract, the Scottish progressive educationalist A.S. Neill offers us a radically different conception of the teacher's disciplinary role. Neill, who went on to establish the well-known democratic school *Summerhill*, wrote *A Dominie's log* in 1915 as a reflective diary of his early years as a teacher.

EXTRACT ONE

Neill, AS (1968) A Dominie's Log: The Story of a Scottish Teacher. *Hogarth Press, pages 15–19*

I have been thinking about discipline overnight. I have seen a headmaster who insisted on what he called perfect discipline. His bairns sat still all day. A movement foreshadowed the strap. Every child jumped up at the word of command. He had a very quiet life.

I must confess that I am an atrociously bad disciplinarian. To-day Violet Brown began to sing Tipperary to herself when I was marking the registers. I looked up and said: "Why the happiness this morning, Violet?" and she blushed and grinned. I am a poor disciplinarian.

I find that normally I am very, very slack; I don't mind if they talk or not. Indeed, if the hum of conversation stops, I feel that something has happened and I invariably look towards the door to see whether an Inspector has arrived.

I find that I am almost a good disciplinarian when my liver is bad; I demand silence then ... but I fear I do not get it, and I generally laugh. The only discipline I ask for usually is the discipline that interest draws. If a boy whets his pencil while I am describing the events that led to the Great Rebellion, I sidetrack him on the topic of rabbits ... and I generally make him sit up. I know that I am teaching badly if the class is loafing, and I am honest enough in my saner moments not to blame the bairns.

I do not like strict discipline, for I do believe that a child should have as much freedom as possible. I want a bairn to be human, and I try to be human myself. I walk to school each morning with my briar between my lips, and if the fill is not smoked, I stand and watch the boys play. I would kiss my wife in my classroom, but ... I do not have a wife. A wee lassie stopped me on the way to school this morning, and she pushed a very sticky sweetie into my hand. I took my pipe from my mouth and ate the sweetie — and I asked for another; she was highly delighted.

Discipline, to me, means a pose on the part of the teacher. It makes him very remote; it lends him dignity. Dignity is a thing I abominate. I suppose the bishop is dignified because he wants to show that there is a real difference between his salaried self and the under-paid curate. Why should I be dignified before my bairns? Will they scorn me if I slide with them? (There was a dandy slide on the road to-day. I gave them half-an-hour's extra play this morning, and I slid all the time. My assistants are adepts at the game.)

But discipline is necessary; there are men known as Inspectors. And Johnny must be flogged if he does not attend to the lesson. He must know the rivers of Russia. After all, why should he? I don't know them, and I don't miss the knowledge. I couldn't tell you the capital of New Zealand ... is it Wellington? or Auckland? I don't know; all I know is that I could find out if I wanted to.

I do not blame Inspectors. Some of them are men with what I would call a vision. I had the Chief Inspector of the district in the other day, and I enjoyed his visit. He has a fine taste in poetry, and a sense of humour.

The Scotch Education Department is iniquitous because it is a department; a department cannot have a sense of humour. And it is humour that makes a man decent and kind and human.

If the Scotch Education Department were to die suddenly I should suddenly become a worse disciplinarian than I am now. If Willie did not like Woodwork, I should say to him: "All right, Willie. Go and do what you do like, but take my advice and do some work; you will enjoy your football all the better for it."

I believe in discipline, but it is self-discipline that I believe in. I think I can say that I never learned anything by being forced to learn it, but I may be wrong. I was forced to learn the Shorter Catechism, and today I hate the sight of it. I read the other day in Barrie's Sentimental Tommy *that its meaning comes to one long afterwards and at a time when one is most in need of it. I confess that the time has not come for me; it will never come, for I don't remember two lines of the Catechism.*

It is a fallacy that the nastiest medicines are the most efficacious; Epsom Salts are not more beneficial than Syrup of Figs.

A thought! ... If I believe in self-discipline, why not persuade Willie that Woodwork is good for him as a self-discipline? Because it isn't my job. If Willie dislikes chisels he will always dislike them. What I might do is this: tell him to persevere with his chisels so that he might cut himself badly. Then he might discover that his true vocation is bandaging, and straightway go in for medicine.

Would Willie run away and play at horses if I told him to do what he liked best? I do not think so. He likes school, and I think he likes me. I think he would try to please me if he could.

In his classroom, Neill states that the discipline he seeks is the discipline that interest draws.

- *What does he mean by this?*

- *What are the benefits and limitations of this approach to discipline?*

- *What are your views on Neill's contention that teachers should not be remote and dignified from their pupils?*

Extract one illustrates Neill's preference for internal self-discipline. He believed that teacher-imposed discipline has the effect of obstructing the development of such self-discipline. Rather he argued that children should be free to make choices about what and how they learn. From his perspective, disruptive behaviour is a response to coercive pedagogies and to the unhappiness caused by teachers imposing an adult conception of childhood on the pupils that they teach. Paradoxically, from Neill's perspective, teachers create poor discipline in the very act of disciplining pupils to do things they don't want to do!

The changing face of teacher professionalism

In many ways, Neill's pedagogical approach seems a long way from the expectations on teachers in schools today and, if he were alive to see it, he would be pretty horrified. Firstly, he would detest the extent that the modern teacher is monitored – by government agencies and through a range of performance indicators (including pupil attainment and retention rates, classroom observation, absence and course feedback). Secondly, he would dislike the way that the teacher's activities are dictated by content- and assessment-heavy curricula, in what has become a centrally prescribed and regulated system. Thirdly, he would abhor the competition that has come to characterise education over the last 20 years.

Since the 1980s, government reforms have significantly altered the working lives of teachers and changed the way we understand teachers' professional identity (Day and Smethem, 2009). In the following extract, Whitty points to a number of factors that have impacted on the role of the teacher in recent years, including:

- an emphasis on measurable performance indicators – 'performativity';

- increased decision-making power at the level of the school;

- a business ethos in education, placing an emphasis on organisational efficiency and customer orientation – 'managerialism';

- centralisation of curriculum and assessment;

- marketisation and competition between schools;

- a wider range of stakeholders involved in education.

According to some theorists, these reforms have resulted in a process of 'deprofessionalisation' – brought on by intensification in workload, growth in fractional contracts and the use of teaching agencies, and increasingly regulated and prescribed teaching routines. This has resulted in the loss of autonomy, of independence and of status, and an increased fear of failure and workplace insecurity. From this perspective the role of the teacher has been *deskilled* to such an extent that it can no longer be classified as a profession. Others argue that a *new professionalism* has emerged out of the reforms, defined by adherence to the goals of raising standards and efficiency and by responsiveness and flexibility to market demands, and measured by an increasing numbers of performance indicators (see Shain and Gleeson, 1999 – for an account of this process in further education). The capacity to deliver a service that people want (in an effective, efficient and accountable manner) is what delineates the *professional* teacher today it would seem.

In the following extract, Whitty analyses the changing nature of professionalism in the modern era and offers us an alternative conceptualisation based on democratic engagement and collaboration between the various stakeholders.

EXTRACT TWO

Whitty, G (2006) 'Teacher Professionalism in a New Era'. Paper presented to General Teaching Council, March 2006, pages 1, 2, 14

Contemporary educational reform – including both marketisation and centralisation, but also a new emphasis on the involvement of a wider range of stakeholders – has resulted in a period of significant change for teachers. It has also raised new questions: for example, how should we understand the role of the teacher? Who has a right to be involved in decisions about education? Consequently, and perhaps more than ever in recent times, we need to reflect on the appropriateness of existing notions of teacher professionalism to the context in which teachers work and to the goal of social justice.

Devolution and competition, alongside increasing central prescription and performativity demands, have become global trends in education policy over the past twenty years, even though the particular balance of policies has varied from place to place and, indeed, from government to government within particular countries (Whitty, Power & Halpin, 1998).

Yet, particularly in those countries that embarked early on these reforms, both market-based policies and so-called 'Third Way' alternatives are already demonstrating their limitations, especially in relation to social justice.

In England, the New Labour government has recently admitted that its own research demonstrates this failure: it shows that, although educational standards have risen overall during its term of office, the relative performance of children from poorer socioeconomic backgrounds has not improved (Kelly, 2005). This is despite the fact that some of New Labour's policies had been expected to counter the social inequities that had arisen from the policies of their Conservative predecessors.

This news did not come as a complete surprise to me; as early as 1997 Peter Mortimore and I had warned that research indicated how the sort of school improvement policies then being advocated by New Labour might well have this effect, unless much stronger measures of positive discrimination were introduced (Mortimore & Whitty, 1997). In the same publication, we deplored the way in which many politicians blamed teachers for all the ills of society and failed to recognise the strength of their commitment to educational improvement. We also argued that it was unrealistic to expect teachers alone to overcome the effects of social disadvantage on education.

Yet, there is a real sense in which recent reforms have been a response to perceived failures on the part of teachers. This view is certainly reflected in the 'official' account of reforms in England offered by Michael Barber, the key architect of New Labour's policies (eg, Barber, 2005). He argues that there have been four phases of reform since the 1960s, as follows:

- *Uninformed professionalism – the period prior to the 1980s, often regarded as the golden age of teacher autonomy but when, according to Barber, teachers lacked appropriate knowledge, skills and attitudes for a modern society*

- *Uninformed prescription – the period following the election of Margaret Thatcher's Conservative government in 1979 and, in particular, its imposition of a National Curriculum in 1988 for political rather than educational reasons*

- *Informed prescription – the period following the election of Tony Blair's New Labour government in 1997, bringing with it (in Barber's view) 'evidence-based' policies such as the Literacy and Numeracy Strategies and Standards-based teacher training*

- *Informed professionalism – a new phase, just beginning, when teachers will have appropriate knowledge, skills and attitudes so that the government can grant them a greater degree of licensed autonomy to manage their own affairs.*

[...] In my view, genuine stakeholder involvement should be welcomed by the professions and the democratisation of professionalism should be adopted as an alternative to both the traditional professional project and the managerialist professional project currently promulgated by governments. A democratic professionalism would seek to demystify professional work and build alliances between teachers and other members of the school workforce, such as teaching assistants, and external stakeholders, including students, parents and members of the wider community. For many of these groups, and particularly marginalised sub-sets of them, decisions will have traditionally been made on their behalf either by professions or the state (Apple, 1996).

If teachers are to make a real contribution to the equity agenda as well as the standards agenda, they must work actively with others committed to teaching for a just society (Gale & Densmore, 2000; 2003). A democratic professionalism thus encourages the development of collaborative cultures in the broadest sense, rather than exclusive ones. It certainly suggests that the teacher has a responsibility that extends beyond the single classroom – including contributing to the school, other students and the wider educational system, as well as to the collective responsibilities of teachers themselves to a broader social agenda. Indeed, under democratic professionalism, this broader agenda becomes part and parcel of the professional agenda rather than being counterposed to it.

EXTRACT TWO *continued*

Sachs' (2003) notion of an 'activist identity' for teachers goes some way towards recog-nising this. Her activist professional works collectively towards strategic ends, operates on the basis of developing networks and alliances between bureaucracies, unions, pro-fessional associations and community organisations. These alliances are not static, but form and are reformed around different issues and concerns. Activist professionals take responsibility for their own on-going professional learning, and work within multiple communities of practice. These develop in larger contexts – historical, social, cultural, institutional (181, see also Sachs, 2001).

POINTS TO CONSIDER

- *You can see from extract two that professionalism, especially within the contexts of education, is a contested concept – it is used to mean different things. Make a list of the characteristics of each of the following:*
    - *uninformed professionalism;*
    - *informed professionalism;*
    - *prescribed professionalism;*
    - *democratic professionalism;*
    - *activist professionalism.*
- *Which meaning fits best with your understanding of teachers' professionalism? Why?*
- *Do you think Barber is correct to suggest that we are moving away from prescription toward more informed professionalism – with a greater degree of teacher autonomy?*
- *How persuasive is Whitty's argument that we need to redefine teacher professionalism along democratic lines if we are to tackle educational inequalities?*

In the 'noughties', government-led initiatives have further compounded a definitive char-acterisation of teacher professionalism: an expectation for teachers to take on wider pastoral and safeguarding roles (as part of the Every Child Matters agenda), reductions in National Tests and the introduction of 14–19 diplomas – with a potential school leaving age of 18 after 2013, expectations for more young people to go into further and higher education, massive increases in funding for resources and buildings, new mobile and inter-active information and communications technologies, guaranteed non-teaching time and, perhaps most significantly, an increase in the number of teaching assistants and learning support in the classroom (see Baker, 2009). Teachers certainly need to be adaptive in this continuously changing policy landscape.

It is difficult to assess whether the sum of these changes has impacted positively or nega-tively on teachers today. It is easy to see how such a fluid environment can result in high levels of pressure – and evidence informs us that teachers are more likely than people in many occupations to report high levels of work-related stress. Managerialist and performativity cultures certainly undermine the capacity for teachers to shape their own working lives. But increases in pay and pledges to reduce the bureaucratic and monitoring burdens and curriculum and assessment improve the status and appeal of teaching. Recent evidence also suggests that new recruits to teaching are more receptive to, and willing to engage with, the *new professionalism* of performance, assessment and target-setting (Storey, 2007).

Teaching in the real world: from policy to practice

Questions concerning the nature of teacher professionalism elucidate a potential for division between the objectives of policy makers and the experiences of practitioners *on the ground*. Policies intended to raise standards and promote efficiency are frequently perceived and experienced as increasing the workload and obstructing effective learning and teaching. This distinction is made very clear in Michael Apple's account of his teaching experiences with a pupil, Joseph.

EXTRACT THREE

Apple, M (2009) "Is There a Place for Education in Social Transformation" in Svi Shapiro, H. (2009) Education and Hope in Troubled Times: Sociocultural, Political and Historical Studies in Education Studies. *Routledge, pages 31–32*

Joseph sobbed at my desk. He was a tough kid, a hard case, someone who often made life difficult for his teachers. He was all of nine years old and here he was sobbing, holding on to me in public. He had been in my fourth-grade class all year, a classroom situated in a decaying building in an east coast city that was among the most impoverished in the nation. There were times when I wondered, seriously, whether I would make it through that year. There were many Josephs in that classroom and I was constantly drained by the demands, the bureaucratic rules, the daily lessons that bounced off of the kids' armor. Yet somehow it was satisfying, compelling and important, even though the prescribed curriculum and the textbooks that were meant to teach it were often beside the point. They were boring to the kids and boring to me.

I should have realized the first day what it would be like when I opened that city's 'Getting Started' suggested lessons for the first few days and it began with the suggestion that, 'as a new teacher,' I should circle the students' desks and have them introduce each other and tell something about themselves. It's not that I was against this activity; it's just that I didn't have enough unbroken desks (or even chairs) for all of the students. A number of the kids had nowhere to sit. This was my first lesson – but certainly not my last – in understanding that the curriculum and those who planned it lived in an unreal world, a world fundamentally disconnected from my life with those children in that inner-city classroom.

But here's Joseph. He's still crying. I've worked extremely hard with him all year long. We've eaten lunch together; we've read stories we've gotten to know each other. There

---

are times when he drives me to despair and other times when I find him among the most sensitive children in my class. I just can't give up on this kid. He's just received his report card and it says that he is to repeat his fourth grade. The school system has a policy that states that failure in any two subjects (including the 'behavior' side of the report card) requires that the student be left back. Joseph was failing 'gym' and arithmetic. Even though he had shown improvement, he had trouble keeping awake during arithmetic, had done poorly on the mandatory city-wide tests, and hated gym. One of his parents worked a late shift and Joseph would often stay up, hoping to spend some time with her. And the things that students were asked to do in gym were, to him, 'lame'.

The thing is, he had made real progress during the year. But I was instructed to keep him back. I knew that things would be worse next year. There would still not be enough desks. The poverty in that community would still be horrible and health care and sufficient funding for job training and other services would be diminished. I knew that the jobs that were available in this former mill town paid deplorable wages and that, even with both his parents working for pay, Joseph's family income was simply insufficient. I also knew that, given all that I already had to do each day in that classroom and each night at home in preparation for the next day, it would be nearly impossible for me to work any harder than I had already done with Joseph. And there were another five children in that class whom I was supposed to leave back.

So Joseph sobbed. Both he and I understood what this meant. There would be no additional help for me – or for children such as Joseph – next year. The promises would remain simply rhetorical. Words would be thrown at the problems. Teachers and parents and children would be blamed. But the school system would look like it believed in and enforced higher standards. The structuring of economic and political power in that community and that state would again go on as 'business as usual'.

The next year Joseph basically stopped trying. The last time I heard anything about him was that he was in prison.

This story is not apocryphal. While the incident took place a while ago, the conditions in that community and that school are much worse today. And the intense pressure that teachers, administrators and local communities are under is also considerably worse (Kozol 1991; Lipman 2004). It reminds me of why large numbers of thoughtful educators and activists mistrust the incessant focus on standards, increased testing, marketization and vouchers, and other kinds of educational 'reforms' which may sound good in the abstract, but which often work in exactly the opposite ways when they reach the level of the classroom (see Apple 2006; Valenzuela 2005; Lipman 2004; McNeil 2000). It is exactly this sensibility of the contradictions between proposals for reform and the realities and complexities of education on the ground that provides one of the major reasons so many of us are asking the questions surrounding how education can make a more serious contribution to social justice.

POINTS TO CONSIDER

- *Apple talks of a fundamental disconnection between policy makers and the experiences of teachers in the classroom. What strategies might start to make connections between these two worlds?*

- *Why might an increased focus on standards and testing impact negatively on students like Joseph?*

- *Within the current education system, what kinds of strategies might individual teachers employ to make a difference for children like Joseph?*

Both Apple and Whitty point to the role of the teacher in promoting social justice. They both perceive policy reforms (in the US for Apple) as hindering the capacity for teachers to 'make a difference' to the lives of the children they teach. Apple in particular was influenced by the seminal work of Brazilian educationalist, Paulo Freire, who emphasised the social and political contexts of teaching and viewed education as the means of overcoming oppression (1996). Freire's work was highly prominent in the emergence of an important new theory of teaching, known as 'critical pedagogy' – with proponents including Henry Giroux, Peter McLaren and Michael Apple himself.

Critical pedagogists start from the premise that teachers cannot be neutral – they either support the status quo (and therefore the oppressors) or fight for change (for the oppressed). Advocates of the perspective argue that the teacher's task is to cultivate *critical consciousness* in their students by encouraging them to critique the world that they live in: to question and challenge domination and inequality. Classes need to relate to the real lived experience of each student, aiming to provoke individual and collective action to transform the world. Teachers who adopt the approach of critical pedagogy are frequently criticised for promoting an anti-establishment position rather than allowing students the freedom to make their own minds up. Nevertheless, the theory encourages teachers to think about the impact of what they are doing and to make connections between what goes on in their classroom and the outside world that their students inhabit. It encourages them to reflect on their profession in a moral way – a way that is entirely devoid in the language of standards, targets and efficiency – and to question the teaching of disembodied facts and figures at the same time as many thousands of children are dying as a result of avoidable poverty.

Rethinking teaching in a new world

The final extract is taken from a short but seminal book – 'Teaching as a Subversive Activity'. The central contention of the book is that the education was designed in and for a world that no longer exists. Writing in the late 1960s, Postman and Weingartner had in mind the emergence of mass media, and the resulting explosion in the amount of information people needed to process. They argued that the new media-dominated world was radically different from its predecessors, but that educators had failed to recognise this. Teachers, they contended, transmit knowledge as something that is stable and uncontested, failing to prepare children for a world with rapidly changing information, multiple points of view and ways of life.

While the book was written more than 40 years ago, this central contention is even more apposite today. New information and communication technologies accelerate the speed of change, proliferate the perspectives we have access to, and offer the 'audience' or 'user' the opportunity to participate in, contribute to and generate their own content. So it is still worth reflecting on the changes in the role of the teacher that Postman and Weingartner offered us at the end of the 1960s. In what they call the inquiry method of teaching, they suggest that teachers avoid rigidly prepared lessons, judging students' work or summarising discussions. Rather they promote problem-posing, peer-to-peer communication and asking divergent questions – so that students become less fearful of failure, more confident in their own judgements and less reliant on the viewpoints of others (1971, pages 31–37). They also offer a series of more radical suggestions, as illustrated in the extract.

EXTRACT FOUR

Postman, N and Weingartner, C (1971) Teaching as a Subversive Activity. *Harmondsworth: Penguin Books, pages 134–137*

And so we will now put before you a list of proposals that attempt to change radically the nature of the existing school environment. Most of them will strike you as thoroughly impractical but only because you will have forgotten for the moment that the present system is among the most impractical imaginable, if the facilitation of learning is your aim. There is yet another reaction you might have to our proposals. You might concede that they are 'impractical' and yet feel that each one contains an idea or two that might be translated into 'practical' form. If you do, we will be delighted. But as for us, none of our proposals seems impractical or bizarre. They seem, in fact, quite conservative, given the enormity of the problem they are intended to resolve. As you read them, imagine that you are a member of a board of education, or a principal, or supervisor, or some such person who might have the wish and power to lay the groundwork for a new education.

1. **Declare a five-year moratorium on the use of all textbooks.**
   Since with two or three exceptions all texts are not only boring but based on the assumption that knowledge exists prior to, independent of, and altogether outside of the learner, they are either worthless or harmful. If it is impossible to function without text-books, provide every student with a notebook filled with blank pages, and have him compose his own text.

2. **Have English teachers teach maths, maths teachers English, social studies teachers science, science teachers art and so on.**
   One of the largest obstacles to the establishment of a sound learning environment is the desire of teachers to get something they think they know into the heads of people who don't know it. An English teacher-teaching math would hardly be in a position to fulfill this desire. Even more important, he would be forced to perceive the subject as a learner, not a teacher. If this suggestion is too impractical, try numbers 3 and 4.

3. **Transfer all the elementary-school teachers to high school and vice versa.**

4. *Require every teacher who thinks he knows his subject well to write a book on it.*
   In this way, he will be relieved of the necessity of inflicting his knowledge on other people, particularly his students.

5. *Dissolve all subjects, courses, and especially course requirements.*
   This proposal, all by itself, would work every existing educational bureaucracy. The result would be to deprive teachers of the excuses presently given for their failures and to free than to concentrate on their learners.

6. *Limit each teacher to three declarative sentences per class, and fifteen interrogations.*
   Every sentence above the limit would be subject to a twenty-five-cent fine. The students can do the counting and the collecting.

7. *Prohibit teachers from asking any questions they already know the answers to.*
   This proposal would not only force teachers to perceive learning from the learner's perspective, it would help than to learn how to ask questions that produce knowledge.

8. *Declare a moratorium on all tests and grades.*
   This would remove from the hands of teachers their major weapons of coercion and would eliminate two of the major obstacles to their students' learning anything significant.

9. *Require all teachers to undergo some form of psychotherapy as part of their in-service training.*
   This need not be psychoanalysis; some form of group therapy or psychological counseling will do. Its purpose: to give teachers an opportunity to gain insight into themselves, particularly into the reasons they are teachers.

10. *Classify teachers according to their ability and make the lists public.*
    There would be a 'smart' group (the Bluebirds), an 'average' group (the Robins), and a 'dumb' group (the Sandpipers). The lists would be published each year in the community paper. The IQ and reading scores of teachers would also be published, as well as the list of those who are 'advantaged' and 'disadvantaged' by virtue of what they know in relation to what their students know.

11. *Require all teachers to take a test prepared by students on what the students know.*
    Only if a teacher passes this test should he be permitted to teach. This test could be used for grouping the teachers as in number 10 above.

12. *Make every class an elective and withhold a teacher's monthly cheque if his students do not show any interest in going to next month's classes.*
    This proposal would simply put the teacher on a par with other professionals, e.g. doctors, dentists, lawyers, etc. No one forces you to go to a particular doctor unless you are a 'clinic case'. In that instance, you must take what you are given. Our present system makes a clinic case of every student. Bureaucrats decide who shall govern your

education. *In this proposal, we are restoring the American philosophy: no clients, no money; lots of clients, lots of money.*

13. **Require every teacher to take a one-year leave of absence every fourth year to work in some field other than education.**
    Such an experience can be taken as evidence albeit shaky, that the teacher has been in contact with reality at some point in his life. Recommended occupations: bartender, cab driver, garment worker, waiter. One of the common sources of difficulty with teachers can be found in the fact that most of them simply move from one side of the desk (as students) to the other side (as teachers) and they have not had much contact with the way things are outside of school rooms.

14. **Require each teacher to provide some sort of evidence that he or she has had a loving relationship with at least one other human being.**
    If the teacher can get someone to say,' I love her (or him)' she should be retained. If she can get two people to say it, she should get a raise. Spouses need not be excluded from testifying

15. **Require that all the graffiti accumulated in the school toilets be reproduced on huge paper and be hung in the school halls.**
    Graffiti that concerns teachers and administrators should be chiseled into the stone at the front entrance of the school.

16. **There should be a general prohibition against the use of the following words and phrases:** *teach, syllabus, covering ground, IQ, makeup, test, disadvantaged, gifted, accelerated, enhancement, course, grade, score, human nature, dumb, college material and administrative necessity.*

POINTS TO CONSIDER

- *Consider the merits of each of these recommendations – which ones do you think might be realistic and impact positively on schooling today?*

- *In the list, Postman and Weingartner seem to be suggesting that a teacher's subject expertise can hinder their ability to teach – why might this be and do you agree?*

- *What do you think is the overall notion of teaching reflected in this list of suggestions – try to write a paragraph describing the alternative role of the teacher it recommends.*

- *Try to find instances of alternative approaches to teaching in the current state schooling sector.*

As you have seen earlier in the chapter, the 1970s is often viewed as the period when teachers were most innovative. Prior to the development of the National Curriculum and other forms of centralised control and surveillance in the 1980s, teachers had greater autonomy to think independently about the learning environments they wanted to create.

For many, however, changes in information and communication technology and in the independence of schools have resulted in a climate where teachers might be able to think radically about their teaching again – both in their own classrooms and on a wider scale. David Hargreaves, as Associate Director of the Specialist Schools and Academies Trust, has pioneered the idea of *system redesign* – a series of 'building blocks' to challenge taken-for-granted assumptions and to promote educational innovation (Hargreaves, 2007). He argues that the education system was designed to meet the needs of a previous period and that it requires wholesale innovation to fit more appropriately with the modern world. Rather than being the remit of central government, Hargreaves argues *system redesign* should be placed in the hands of teachers and heads in local school settings. Schools are better positioned than central government to understand the specific contexts – of their unique locations, challenges and pupil intakes. Moreover, he argues, teachers need to think innovatively as part of their daily lives – in response to children's changing needs and demands. So they already possess the skills appropriate to the task of leading substantial change.

You can find a video with examples of *system redesign* from four schools at www.teachers.tv/video/25055. And you can find a full list of the *building blocks for system redesign* on either the International Networking for Educational Transformation (iNet) or Specialist Schools and Academies Trust (SSAT) websites.

Teaching is a tremendously important and rewarding profession. It is also extremely intense and exacting – in terms of workload, physical, social and emotional demands. Teachers are expected to perform multiple (and continuously evolving) roles: with tensions between their roles as disciplinarian and friend/supporter, subject authority and active learning facilitator, meeting the needs of the whole class and the needs of each individual child, and between their own individual professional agency and school and central policy. As you have seen during this chapter, these tensions are most fraught when there is incongruence between a teacher's personal values and those of the wider educational institution/policy discourse.

C H A P T E R   S U M M A R Y

This chapter has provided examples of teachers' reflections on their classroom experience. Both Neill and Apple offer perspectives that are at odds with mainstream policy discourses. They encourage us to reflect on the relationships between teaching and discipline and between policy makers and practitioners. Whitty asks us to interrogate how policy initiatives have remodeled professionalism to fit with the standards and 'performativity' agendas, and how teachers might reclaim ownership of it. Postman and Weingartner offer dramatic and seemingly unfeasible ideas for transformation – but by reading them you start to see the assumptions that underpin our understanding of the teacher today. You may have even been persuaded by a few of their suggestions. All the readings ask us to (re)consider what teaching is really all about.

REFERENCES

Baker, M (2009) 'Educational Review of the Decade'. BBC website (30/12/09) **http://news.bbc. co.uk/1/hi/education/8421554.stm**

Day, C and Smethem, L. (2009) The effects of reform: Have teachers really lost their sense of professionalism? *Journal of educational change*, 10, pp141–157

DCSF (2009) *School discipline: Your powers and rights as a teacher.* DCSF/NASUWT

Freire, P (1996) *Pedagogy of the oppressed*. Harmondsworth: Penguin Books

Hargreaves, D (2007) *System redesign 1 – the road to transformation in education*. Specialist Schools and Academies Trust

Shain, F and Gleeson, D (1999) Teachers' work and professionalism in the further education sector. *Education and Social Justice*, 1 (3), pp55–63

Steer, A (2009) *Learning behaviour: lessons learned, a review of behaviour standards and practices in our schools*. DCSF

Storey, A (2007) Cultural shifts in teaching: new workforce, new professionalism. *Curriculum journal*, 18(3), pp253–270, September 2007

Wardrop, M (2009) Badly behaved pupils should be given a "right royal rollicking", says Sir Alan Steer. *The Daily Telegraph*. www.telegraph.co.uk, 05/05/09

Darder, A, Baltodano, M and Torres, R (ed.) (2008) *The critical pedagogy reader*. (2nd edition). London: Routledge

Galton, M and MacBeath, J (2008) *Teachers under pressure*. London: Sage Publications

Gewirtz, S, Mahony, P, Hextall, I and Cribb, A (ed.) (2008) *Changing teacher professionalism: international trends, challenges and ways forward*. London: Routledge

Johnson, D and Maclean, R (ed.) (2008) *Teaching: professionalism, development and leadership*. Dordrecht, Netherlands: Springer

Pollard, A (2008) *Reflective teaching: evidence-informed professional practice*. London: Continuum

http://uk.partnersinlearningnetwork.com/Pages/default.aspx

www.teachers.tv/

www.tda.gov.uk/

www.radicalteacher.org/

Chapter 3
Curriculum and assessment

OBJECTIVES

By the end of this chapter you should have:
- identified and evaluated a range of approaches to understanding and modelling the curriculum;
- discussed the advantages and disadvantages of dividing the school curriculum into distinct subjects;
- considered why the examination is such a central component of assessment in schools today and what this tells us about the purpose of education;
- critically assessed alternative conceptions of assessment and curriculum.

Introduction

This chapter examines two centrally important concepts in today's formal educational settings – *curriculum* and *assessment* – and shows how both can be used to organise, structure and construct particular ways of thinking about learning, knowledge and relationships between teachers and students in schools.

The chapter considers the argument that neither curriculum nor assessment are neutral or value-free concepts, but that both can in fact be seen as powerful tools for ordering, classifying and attributing value, both to people and to ideas. A secondary school curriculum, for example, is likely to be ordered into distinct and discretely timetabled subjects – through which students learn that doing history is different from doing English, or doing chemistry. These distinctions might seem obvious and/or inevitable but writers such as Ball and Goodson (1984) urge us to think of school subjects as social and political constructions, the product of ongoing and historical contest, struggle and debate. Within a school timetable, some subjects may be awarded higher status than others in the eyes of teachers, students, parents or potential employers. This could be reflected in the allocation of total teaching hours or financial resources or whether the study of a particular subject is made compulsory for all students or not. Within an individual subject area, certain topics are chosen for inclusion while others may be left out entirely: which works should be studied in a course on English literature, for example? Would it matter if white, middle-class, British men wrote the only available course texts? End of unit assessments also depend on judgements about which answers, which accounts or which interpretations are 'right' within this context and therefore which students will receive A-grades and which students will fail.

What do we mean by curriculum?

The term 'curriculum' is used and understood within Education Studies and popular discussion in a variety of different ways. For some, curriculum is used rather narrowly to refer to a list of subjects or items to be taught (we could also think of the terms 'syllabus' or 'specification' here). For others, it is important to understand the curriculum as much more than that. Kerr for example defines the curriculum as *all the learning which is planned and guided by the school, whether it is carried on in groups or individually, inside or outside the school* (1968, page 16) while Jenkins and Shipman suggest *a curriculum is the formulation and implementation of an educational proposal to be taught and learned within a school or other institution and for which that institution accepts responsibility at three levels, its rationale, its actual implementation and its effects* (cited in Neary, 2002, pages 34–35).

Jenkins and Shipman's definition is useful because it draws attention to the different levels on which a curriculum could be seen to operate: *rationale*, *implementation* and *effects*.

Rationale

In terms of *rationale* we could think of a formal, written curriculum – as might appear in official policy documents, for example – and consider what aims or outcomes the authors intend to achieve. White describes the curriculum *as a vehicle, or collection of vehicles, intended to reach a certain set of destinations* (2004, page 6). Sometimes the aims, objectives, or intended destination of a curriculum are stated openly. The current National Curriculum for England, for example, begins by explaining that:

> *The curriculum should enable all young people to become:*
>
> - *successful learners who enjoy learning, make progress and achieve;*
>
> - *confident individuals who are able to live safe, healthy and fulfilling lives;*
>
> - *responsible citizens who make a positive contribution to society.*
>
> (QCDA, 2010)

In other contexts, intended aims and desirable outcomes are left implicit and more critical questioning and consideration might be needed to interpret what the creators of a particular curriculum are hoping to achieve.

Implementation

Implementation focuses on the curriculum in practice, as it is actually interpreted and enacted by individual teachers and students in schools. A curriculum might consist of a tightly prescribed, comprehensive list of instructions or it might offer only a general framework within which there is considerable scope for interpretation, innovation or change. In either case there is no guarantee that any official, written documentation will be implemented in practice exactly as its initial authors had intended: teaching and learning are dynamic and not always predictable activities.

Effects

Any curriculum is likely to have both intended and unintended – predictable and unexpected – consequences. These consequences are likely to vary considerably between different people or groups of people. It is important to recognise that not all learning that takes place is ever formally written down. You may have heard the expression, *the hidden curriculum* which some writers use to describe the informal and/or unofficial 'lessons' that students are likely to pick up on while in school. Learning to wait quietly with a hand-raised before being invited to make a contribution by a teacher, competing for end-of-term merit or house points for good behaviour or sporting prowess, playing in the year 7/8 only section of the playground are all activities which impart messages about how it is considered appropriate for young people to behave.

Competing models for the curriculum

Now that you have been introduced to some of the variety of explanations offered to help understand what the curriculum *is*, it perhaps won't surprise you to read that there is also considerable debate and disagreement as to how a curriculum should be constructed. Four alternative models for approaching curriculum theory are outlined below. As you will see, each depends on rather different understandings of what is arguably the most fundamental educational question: what is education for?

Model 1: Curriculum as transmission

The oldest and perhaps most traditional model for a curriculum is as a list of knowledge to be imparted from teachers to students. Education, as the process of acquiring knowledge, is presented as having intrinsic value: no other justification is needed. Here, questions about the curriculum are questions about *content*: what knowledge is most important to present to students in schools. There is a clear hierarchical relationship between teachers and students: teachers possess this knowledge and learners do not. But who decides which content to include?

Model 2: Curriculum as product

A second, currently very widespread, model of curriculum shifts focus from questions of content to questions concerning the sorts of students that a curriculum might help to produce. Here, what a student knows is no longer as important in its own right as what a student is able to do: the content and structure of a curriculum is decided and developed in order to achieve a specific end. Knowledge (of mathematics or of history or of literature) is no longer considered valuable in its own right but only as it helps students to become more useful members of the workforce or better citizens. Successful teaching and learning is defined by the extent that students are able to demonstrate acquisition of specific competencies. This model of curriculum is most closely associated with the work of Ralph Tyler (1949) but it has come under considerable criticism. A common argument is that teachers become little more than 'technicians' – told exactly what they must do and how to do it with limited opportunity for imagination or creativity.

Model 3: Curriculum as process

Unlike the previous two models, here learners are given agency – they are not just seen as objects to which education happens, but individuals who interact with teachers, make their own judgements and interpretations, and contributing to their own experience, knowledge and understanding. Famously advocated by Lawrence Stenhouse (1974), this model emphasises strategies of teaching and the process of learning, not simply the content of the curriculum or the end product it achieves. This is not to say that those who subscribe to a process model of curriculum are not concerned with the skills, attitudes and behaviours of students who leave school, it is just that for them the means are as important as the ends. Moreover, this perspective says that you cannot and should not want to entirely predict the outcome of an educational encounter: there needs to be room for surprise, innovation, creativity and change. The process model has been criticised for being harder to measure than the previous two models. It places great importance on the skills of each individual teacher, so is dependent on high-quality teacher training, support and continuing professional development.

Model 4: Curriculum as praxis

The praxis model of curriculum developed out of the process model. Evident in the work of critical pedagogy theorists (see Giroux, 1988), it has social transformation and the relationship between theory and practice as its chief concerns. At the other extreme from transmission, the praxis model conceives of knowledge as tentative and open to critique: often challenging taken-for-granted knowledge as the voice of the powerful and the source of oppression. According to this model, a curriculum is only worthwhile in as much as it has direct relevance to the real lives and experiences of learners. The aim of the praxis model is to raise critical consciousness: the cultivation of informed and committed action as a foundation for hope in the future. Critics argue that this model risks representing to learners a partial and overly critical standpoint on the world.

Curriculum controversies

As you can see then, curriculum is far from straightforward. Curricula are not neutral and purely objective creations. Rather, each is built upon specific understandings of what education is for and what it is important for young people to know and learn. As a result, there is significant disagreement about what should and should not be included. Since its implementation in 1988, the National Curriculum has been the subject of numerous consultations and revisions. Among current curriculum disputes are the following:

- Should sex education be a compulsory part of the National Curriculum? Should some learners be excused from studying it on religious grounds? What should be included in it? At what stage of schooling?

- Should all children have a religious education? Can faith schools teach a different RE curriculum to other schools? What content is/is not included? Is it possible to opt out? Is it OK to teach creationism as part of a science curriculum?

- Should there be a centrally prescribed and regulated National Curriculum? If so, who should write it and who should be consulted? How prescriptive should it be – should schools and teachers have some autonomy over what and how it is delivered? Should different schools be able to study different curricula? For example, is there any problem with the fact that private schools and some state schools can choose, while the majority of schools must teach GCSE? Should there be a National Curriculum for children under the age of 5, as in the Early Years Foundation Stage?

- Are some subject specifications more demanding than others? Some argue that the decline in numbers studying science and mathematics is because these are more difficult than so-called 'soft' subjects. How can there be parity between such different subjects?

- Should subjects like PSHE (Personal, Social and Health Education) and Citizenship be part of the National Curriculum? How should they be learnt and taught? What content should be included in them?

- How far can a prescribed curriculum enable a truly inclusive, differentiated and *personalised* learning experience?

- Is the National Curriculum being 'dumbed down'? Is it easier to achieve high grades than it used to be?

- In its present form, is the curriculum adequately preparing young people for life in the twenty-first century?

The following two extracts were both written in response to the most recent National Curriculum for England's secondary schools. In both cases the authors offer criticisms and/or suggestions for improvements but each from a rather different point of view.

EXTRACT ONE

Woodhead, C (2009) A Desolation of Learning: Is this the Education our Children Deserve? *Pencil Sharp Publishing Ltd, pages 94–96*

The importance of knowledge

My objections to this new National Curriculum are, I hope, clear. In a sentence, those responsible for it are more interested in promulgating political views than they are in teaching academic knowledge. The key criterion in deciding what should be taught appears to be the 'relevance' of the topic to the child's interests as a child and to his or her responsibilities (though this is a word which is used infrequently) as an adult living in a 'diverse' society as a 'global citizen'; the underlying belief is that it is more important to teach children 'how to learn' than it is to open their eyes to the magic and mystery of the world that lies beyond their immediate experience. A curriculum that starts from the 'whole person' aim that children should become 'successful learners, confident individuals, and responsible citizens' is bound to result in a set of requirements that is anti-educational in these ways.

So much, to me, at least, is obvious. Why, though, do I think the mastery of different forms of knowledge important?

...[W]hat we see depends on what we know; and the more we know, the richer our lives. 'The educational engagement is necessary', as Michael Oakeshott states, 'because nobody is born a human being, and because the quality of being human is not a latency which becomes an actuality in a process of "growth".' If we deny our children the opportunity to participate in what Oakeshott calls 'the conversation of mankind', we deny them their humanity.

This is the crucial importance of the subject disciplines and the reason why the arguments of those who, for whatever reason, want to undermine the importance of subject knowledge need to be defeated. The most common objection to this concept of education is that it results in classrooms in which children are spoon-fed facts. I do not for one moment deny that there are such classrooms, but I blame the teachers who use the spoon, not the approach to education, which, in their laziness and incompetence, they bring in to disrepute. It is important, moreover, to note that the conversations of mankind involve forms of knowledge that have nothing to do with fact. Why should all children have the chance to experience great literature? Because, read attentively, poems and novels and plays quicken the pulse of our emotional life. 'Love', 'hate', 'jealousy', 'envy', 'anxiety', 'remorse': the words we use to define our feelings sink into the cliché of everyday use. We think we know what they mean, but we do not. As a consequence, our lives are deadened and diminished.

[...] used the word 'attention' twice in the previous paragraph. 'By understanding', Geoffrey Hill wrote in The Triumph of Love, *the poem from which the epigraph to this book is taken:*

> *'. . . I understand diligence*
>
> *and attention, appropriately understood*
>
> *as actuated self-knowledge, a daily acknowledgement*
>
> *of what is owed the dead'.*

'Diligence and attention': how else are the 'forms of understanding upon which our humanity depends' to be understood? Through a 'personalised' curriculum, which subordinates the mastery of what is difficult to the whim of the individual student? Through programmes of study for the national curriculum subjects which have been bent to the political will? Through a pedagogy that encourages children to value their own opinions over the wisdom of the dead? Elsewhere in his poem, Hill refers to 'these strange children/ pitless in their ignorance and contempt'. England, he writes, has become a nation with 'many memorials but no memory'. He is referring specifically to the forgotten heroism of men who died in the Second World War, but his lament about memory, which is a powerful theme throughout the poem, is more general. These children value nothing because they know nothing. They have no sense of how our knowledge of ourselves depends, as Hill's wordplay points out, upon 'a daily acknowledgement/ of what is owed to the dead'. Neither do the ministers who are ultimately responsible for this strange new curriculum.

EXTRACT ONE *continued*

Like Hill, I believe that 'forms of understanding', such as history and mathematics and lit-erature, are 'far from despicable'. I believe that the fulfillment of our potential as human beings depends on our struggle to engage with and understand these forms. I believe that knowledge and respect are to be preferred to ignorance and contempt. I do not believe that anything worth knowing can be known without diligence and attention.

1 *'Education: the engagement and its frustration' in Education and the Development of Reason ed. R. F. Dearden, P. H. Hirst, and R. S. Peters (London: Routledge, 1972), pp. 21-2.*

POINTS TO CONSIDER

- *What model(s) of the curriculum do you think Woodhead would most closely agree with?*

- *What are Woodhead's primary objections to the current National Curriculum?*

- *How do you think Woodhead views the relationship between the current curriculum and the country's past and/or possible future?*

- *What do you think about Woodhead's assertion of* I do not believe that anything worth knowing can be known without diligence and attention?

It would not be too controversial to characterise Woodhead's argument here as a conservative critique of the current curriculum and what he regards as the erosion of due reverence and regard for *the wisdom of the dead*, or traditional bodies of knowledge (see also Young 2008). A very different perspective is offered in extract two by the authors of Opening Minds, a competence-based curriculum, aimed particularly at Key Stage 3 learners, and focusing on competencies in learning, managing information, relating to people, managing situations and citizenship. For these authors, concern for the future rather than respect for the past is key. As they explain on their website *it is estimated that the top 10 in-demand jobs of 2010 did not exist in 2004. We are currently preparing students for jobs that do not exist!* (RSA, 2010).

EXTRACT TWO

RSA (1999) – 'Opening Minds: Education for the 21st Century' – available at www.thersa.org/projects/education/opening-minds pages 13,17,18

We believe that our work has made the case for a radical restructuring of schooling, and uncovered a substantial volume of support for a long-term change strategy built on a new philosophy of curriculum. The plans we have outlined are intended to put in place a curriculum model that would do more, perhaps, than anything else to produce the right answer to our starting questions: what should education look like in twenty years' time? how should we be preparing young people for the future?

EXTRACT TWO *continued*

The vision that underpins the RSA's proposal is clear. We want an education system that will help every young person develop to the best of his or her ability the competences needed to become a successful, active citizen; to be able to contribute their creative and other talents to their work, their families and to society. We want them to understand why every aspect of their education is important and why they are being asked to prepare themselves for adult life in a particular way; that their education is about both essential competences and developing their capacity to enjoy life and to value learning for its own sake.

[...] there was a wish that the framework should find some way of reflecting and valuing the different ways in which students learn, as well as stating what they are expected to learn; and that there should be constant emphasis on what should be learnt, rather than on teaching. The contrast was made with the programmes of study within the present National Curriculum, which are expressed primarily in terms of what is to be taught. There are limitations on what can be done at the level of the overall framework, but again the final revision attempts to reflect this wish. There is nothing in it to prescribe any particular style of teaching or learning; on the contrary, we think the framework would open up to teachers a wide and proper scope for the use of their professional judgement.

[...] the most contentious issues raised concerned the relationship between a compe-tence-led curriculum and subject content. The RSA curriculum would rely on the careful deployment of what is generally termed subject content as the medium through which competences are developed. It would be the development by students of the compe-tences, rather than the acquisition of subject knowledge, which would be assessed at appropriate stages. How the relationship between the two should be managed is a com-plex issue and raises questions both of principle and practice.

There are clearly some in education who cannot envisage a curriculum organised other than on a traditional subject basis. They point to the subject orientation of teachers, to perceived difficulty in delivery and to public familiarity with subject organisation as reasons why the RSA model is impractical or unacceptable. But these are contingent argu-ments rather than points of principle. They did not strike us as especially strong; the RSA is looking a decade or two ahead as the period over which a new curriculum model would be developed and introduced, a period over which these important questions could be addressed. The main objections of principle appear to reflect a fixed view that the pur-pose of education is the transmission of a corpus of knowledge and not the inculcation of particular attitudes or behaviours. Yet every school is in practice active in the latter, as is evidenced from their statements of values.

[...] These varying viewpoints must be contrasted with the strong support we have received from many individuals and organisations, within and beyond the education serv-ice, for achieving strategic change through a competence-led curriculum. Some stemmed from disillusion with the ability of the present curriculum to engage many young people and a belief that it is of declining relevance and usefulness as the world beyond education changes. This is reinforced by the growing difficulty of convincing some students of its value and relevance, especially when employers are voicing disillusion with the quality and

nature of the educational attainments of new entrants to the labour market, regardless of level. A very strong view was expressed that the domination of traditional subject content was so strong that no attempt to graft competence outcomes onto it could ever be successful; this would be true both of teaching and assessment. Only a complete break and the introduction of a new curriculum philosophy would secure the desired results.

POINTS TO CONSIDER

- *Why do you think curricula are typically organised into distinct subject areas? Are there any disadvantages with this approach?*

- *Have a look at the Competences for Learning in the Opening Minds Curriculum – you can find this on the RSA website or on page 18 of the document that this extract is taken from:*

  - *What do you see as the main similarities and differences with the National Curriculum?*

  - *How would you feel as a teacher if you were given this curriculum rather than one based on subject content?*

  - *How would you teach children to have learned, systematically, to think?*

  - *Do you think it is easier to differentiate and to personalise learning with a competence-based or a subject-based curriculum? Why?*

One of the biggest differences between the two perspectives is the authors' perspective on disciplinary/subject boundaries. Woodhead believes the current national curriculum does too much to erode the distinctions between different subjects (i.e. through promoting cross-curricular themes). Conversely the RSA claim that, by focusing on specific content that must be delivered, the subject-centred curriculum *neglects the development of the competences and skills that young people will need to survive and succeed in their future world.* (RSA, 2010).

Woodhead, and many others, argue for the importance of distinct subjects: that each is worth something in its own right. Every discipline has a different logic, teaching different skills and perspectives – there is something inherent in mathematics that is discrete from physics, French or history. From this perspective, the Opening Minds curriculum, along with other models that replace a traditional subject-centred approach with competences, skills or dispositions, fails to provide an appropriate academic learning environment. Commentators are critical, for instance, that Opening Minds involves teachers teaching subjects that they have no specialism in: Ofsted reported that teachers lack *the subject knowledge or skills they need to implement the college's thematic lessons successfully* and that the curriculum fails to *provide enough academic challenge or allow students to achieve as well as they can in individual subjects* (cited in Stewart, 2008).

Others disagree. Returning to the analogy of curriculum as vehicle for arriving at educational destination, White suggests that traditionally distinguished school subjects are themselves, *after all, only vehicles to achieve certain ends: they are not self-justifying entities* (2004, page 6). Could overarching educational aims be realised by other kinds of curricular vehicle? White suggests that familiar subjects are included in most school curricula throughout the world because it is *taken as read that these are what the school curriculum must consist of (ibid.)*. He goes on to record that there was little rationale offered for the particular set of subjects which comprised the first English National Curriculum in 1988: English, mathematics, science, technology, geography, a modern foreign language, music, art, physical education – that these only became cemented as recognisable subjects in late nineteenth and early twentieth centuries. As we move further into the twenty-first century, it is entirely plausible that certain subjects, if not the whole principle of subject-centred curricula, have become outmoded and overly restrictive.

Assessment

If curriculum is concerned with ordering and classifying hierarchies of knowledge, assessment is, in large part, concerned with ordering and classifying individual learners. This is especially true of assessment in its *summative* sense – used to quantify different levels of attainment and to measure how far each learner has achieved the aims of curriculum. Assessment often determines which curriculum learners have access to – one of the most extreme examples of this is the 11+ exam, used to assign places in schools with entirely different curricula. But assessment is also *formative* – used to identify current attainment and need in order to plan future learning and teaching. Formative assessment is about ensuring learners are studying the curriculum at an appropriate level, intensity and pace.

The widespread use of examination

Examination is the form of assessment you will have experienced most during your own education. There are a variety of forms of examination – seen or unseen, multiple choice or essay, written or oral – but all generally share common features: a formal, standardised and supervised setting, set questions or tasks, specified times and places, an external assessor. Exams are perceived to be highly reliable: their standardised nature makes them easier to replicate and administrate across large times and spaces. Anonymous, external marking is seen to minimise the potential for subjective judgments and bias by assessors. With the increase in *high-tech cheating* and stories of parents and teachers providing too much assistance with coursework, exams are seen as a way of reducing the potential for plagiarism and other forms of cheating.

In the third extract, Foucault considers the disciplinary nature of the examination.

Foucault, M (1991) Discipline and Punish: The Birth of the Prison. Penguin Social Sciences, pages 184–185

The examination

The examination combines the techniques of an observing hierarchy and those of a normalizing judgement. It is a normalizing gaze, a surveillance that makes it possible to qualify, to classify and to punish. It establishes over individuals a visibility through which one differentiates them and judges them. That is why, in all the mechanisms of discipline, the examination is highly ritualized. In it are combined the ceremony of power and the form of the experiment, the deployment of force and the establishment of truth. At the heart of the procedures of discipline, it manifests the subjection of those who are perceived as objects and the objectification of those who are subjected. The superimposition of the power relations and knowledge relations assumes in the examination all its visible brilliance. It is yet another innovation of the classical age that the historians of science have left unexplored. People write the history of experiments on those born blind, on wolf-children or under hypnosis. But who will write the more general, more fluid, but also more determinant history of the 'examination' – its rituals, its methods, its characters and their roles, its play of questions and answers, its system of marking and classification? For in this slender technique are to be found a whole domain of knowledge, a whole type of power. One often speaks of the ideology that the human 'sciences' bring with them in either discrete or prolix manner. But does their very technology, this tiny operational schema that has become so widespread (from psychiatry to pedagogy, from the diagnosis of diseases to the hiring of labour), this familiar method of the examination, implement, within a single mechanism, power relations that make it possible to extract and constitute knowledge? It is not simply at the level of consciousness, of representations and in what one thinks one knows, but at the level of what makes possible the knowledge that is transformed into political investment.

- *What do you think Foucault means by the* normalizing gaze *and in what ways does the examination impose this?*

- *Make a list of the* rituals and methods *of the examination – what effects are these likely to have on the examiner and the examined?*

- *What are the associations between the examination, the construction of knowledge and power relations?*

- *Why do you think Foucault perceives the visibility of examination rituals as of particular importance?*

- *How do you think current forms of assessment relate to/constrain the curriculum?*

Compared with their European counterparts, English children experience a large amount of summative assessment (in the form of examinations) during their education. National Tests, GCSE, AS and A2 mean there are few years of study that do not involve formal assessment. Frequently, concerns are raised that the curriculum has become too constrained by assessment overload – that children spend much of their time preparing for assessment and that extended, more active learning opportunities are squeezed. Teachers have reported that they feel pressurised to *teach to the test* (Jozefkowicz, 2006). This has been exacerbated in recent years with the introduction of *high stakes testing* (Wrigley, 2006): whereby assessment results are published in league tables, used to rank individuals and institutions, and used as a basis for the allocation of resources.

Yet, alongside this intensification in summative assessment, there has been a growing recognition of the importance of formative assessment. Assessment for Learning (AfL) and Assessing Pupils' Progress (APP) (DCSF, 2009) are recent initiatives aimed at helping children to recognise their own strengths and weaknesses and to understand how to improve, helping teachers in planning support for learners in reaching their potential, and schools in tracking progression regularly. Initiatives like these highlight assessment as an ongoing, developmental and embedded process at the heart of the learning process.

Innovative assessment

There are many different assessment strategies: observing group work or class contributions, role-plays, oral presentations, simulations, portfolios, diaries or extended projects, to name a few. Technological advances open up all sorts of new alternatives: wikis, discussion boards, blogs, podcasts, films or e-portfolios. These *innovative* assessments can be individual activities or, more radically, can involve a widespread change in assessment mindset. Summative assessments are generally geared around the interests of managers, employers and universities – used to determine which candidates are suitably qualified for employment or further study. For theorists like Heron (1981), innovative assessment is about placing the interests of learners at the centre of assessment practices. He calls for the *redistribution of educational power*: a shift away from assessment 'done to' learners and towards assessment 'done with' or even 'done by' learners. Instead of being excluded from the entire process, as is currently commonplace at all levels of education, Heron argues that learners should be involved at each stage of assessment: writing assessment tasks, defining grading criteria and marking their own and each others' work. Greater use of self and peer assessment, as well as more consultation between learners and teachers, can make assessment fairer, more relevant and can lead to richer and more meaningful learning experiences.

In this final extract, Mohl considers the benefits of innovative assessment in higher education.

EXTRACT FOUR

Mohl, G (2007) 'Innovative Student Assessment'. Deliberations on Teaching and Learning in Higher Education. *London Metropolitan University, pages 6–7*

Cornucopia?

8 possible benefits of innovative assessment

Although many educationalists believe innovative assessment to be a good thing we have to concede that there is, as yet, little research evidence that indicates these benefits are realised in practice. What follows is our collective thoughts on why we feel innovative assessment methods are a good thing for higher education. Some of these thoughts are at present grounded more upon theory than empirical evidence, and whereas they may well be the intended outcomes of innovative assessment, they do not necessarily always represent the actual outcomes.

1. *By incorporating a range of different methods innovative assessment assesses a broader range of skills and as such it is considered to be fairer and less discriminatory. Consequently, innovative assessment should have the effect of widening access to Higher Education and perhaps widening success.*

2. *Innovative assessment is a more reliable assessment of student learning because it is not dependent on any one method of assessment. Innovative assessments allow for the fact that all individuals have strengths and weaknesses, by assessing an individual's performance across a range of skills a more balanced and reliable assessment can be obtained. Don't put all your eggs in one basket!*

3. *Innovative assessment on the whole adopts a more positive approach to education; by spreading the assessment net more widely, it provides students with a range of opportunities to demonstrate how much they understand (Ramsden, 1992), rather than the somewhat negative approach of how little.*

4. *Innovative assessment is usually formative and as such is more likely to facilitate effective, well motivated student learning. Providing timely and constructive feedback allows misunderstandings to be detected and cleared up, and students are able to make improvements where necessary. This process helps maintain student motivation, enabling them to learn more steadily and fluently. If students genuinely don't know what they are doing wrong, as they are never informed, then this can lead to frustration and a loss of interest in the subject.*

5. *A range of different techniques and methods should stimulate both staff and student interest. Variety is the spice of life!*

   Innovative assessment usually means a number of different assessment techniques as opposed to the traditional tutor assessed exams and course work. Although innovative assessment is generally seen as a movement away from examinations, it is not necessarily an end to exams per se, but it is an end to exams in their traditional form. In an innovative form, exam questions may, for example, be revealed beforehand giving students time to prepare a well researched answer, or may emphasise the application

EXTRACT FOUR *continued*

of knowledge to a problem rather than simple memory recall. Unlike traditional assessment, innovative assessment does not rely on exams as a measure of the student's ability, it involves a range of methods and utilises many different media, including: essays, seminars, projects, role plays, simulations, group work, problem solving, presentations, work placements, portfolios, reflective diaries etc.

The assessment itself may also be done by the tutor, by the students, or even by an outsider, such as an employer. Innovative assessment also encourages the assessment of learners not just as individuals but also as individuals working in groups, and as groups of individuals.

6. *Students learn and are assessed upon a much greater variety of skills and in a number of different situations. This should produce more rounded and more employable graduates. Assessments may include students demonstrating that they 'know how to' rather than just 'know about' (Race, 1994).*

7. *Innovative assessment methods are usually more realistic and relevant, involving role plays, simulations and work placements; students develop a better understanding of how their specific skills and knowledge can be applied both inside and outside the academic environment.*

8. *Innovative assessment is generally regarded as a possible strategy for facilitating a 'deep' rather than a 'surface' approach to learning (Marton & Saljo, 1990; Boyd & Cowan, 1985; Ramsden, 1992). Brown & Dove (1993) consulted staff from four different universities who were already using self and peer assessments. The staff reported:* 'students using higher levels of reflection, developing a questioning and self analytic approach to their professional practice and engaging in deep rather than surface learning.' *(Brown & Dove 1993:3)*

POINTS TO CONSIDER

- *Can you see any disadvantages or potential problems with using innovative assessments like those outlined in the extract?*

- *Why might innovative assessments be more likely to facilitate* deep *learning?*

- *Think about the assessment practices on your degree – how far could they be described as innovative? Given the chance, what would you do to change them?*

An example: group assessment

Why is assessment generally conceived of as an individual activity? If you accept that learning is at its most productive and engaging in groups, then why not assess in groups as well? Presentations or extended team projects are excellent strategies for group assessment. And wikis provide a new and exciting way of producing genuinely collaborative work. As formative assessment, group work clearly has benefits: working as a member of a team increases communication and other interpersonal skills, and develops critical thinking. As summative assessment, group tasks have been shown to reduce test anxiety and incidences of cheating (Horton, 2008). One potential difficulty is that group assessments are more able to provide group rather than individual marks – that individuals might find it difficult to present their own work as part of a group. But Horton uses the metaphor of jazz musicians to argue that individuals can excel as part of a group: enabling them to bounce ideas off one another, to experiment, improvise and innovate in developing their own final document.

C H A P T E R   S U M M A R Y

This chapter has introduced you to two core educational concepts – curriculum and assessment. The first two extracts offered competing perspectives on the National Curriculum and the notion of a subject-centred curriculum. An alternative competence-based Opening Minds curriculum was presented and discussed. The chapter then reflected on assessment – questioning the dominance of examination as a way of measuring attainment. It considered alternative *innovative* assessments, arguing that, when planned and implemented effectively, these have the potential to facilitate more engaging, collaborative and *deep* learning experiences.

REFERENCES

Ball, S and Goodson, I (eds) (1984) *Defining the curriculum: histories and ethnographies.* London: Falmer Press

DCSF (2009) *AfL with APP: developing collaborative school-based approaches: Guidance for senior leaders.* DCSF: The National Strategies

Giroux, H (1988) *Teachers as intellectuals: towards a critical pedagogy of learning.* Westport: Bergen and Garvey publishers

Heron, J (1981) 'Assessment revisited', in Boud, D. (ed.) *Developing student autonomy in learning.* London: Kogan Page

Horton, S (2008) 'Lev goes to college: reflections on implementing Vygotsky's ideas in higher education', *International Journal of Learning*, 15 (4) pp. 13–18

Jozefkowicz, E (2006) 'Too many teachers "teaching to the test" '. *The Guardian*, 20 July, 2006

Kerr, J (ed.) (1968) *Changing the curriculum.* London: London University Press

Neary, M (2002) *Curriculum studies in post-compulsory and adult education: a teacher's and student teacher's study guide.* Cheltenham: Nelson Thornes

QCDA (2010) *The aims of the curriculum.* http://curriculum.qcda.gov.uk/uploads/Curriculum%20aims_tcm8-15741.pdf

Stenhouse, L (1974) *An Introduction to curriculum research and development.* London: Heinemann

Stewart (2008) 'Themed lessons get Ofsted thumbs down' *Times Educational Supplement*, 14th November, 2008

Tyler, R (1949) *Basic principles of curriculum and instruction.* Chicago: University of Chicago Press

White, J (ed.) (2004) *Rethinking the school curriculum: values, aims and purposes.* Abingdon: RoutledgeFalmer

Wrigley, T (2006) *Another school is possible*. London: Bookmarks

Young, M (2008) *Bringing knowledge back in: from social constructivism to social realism in the sociology of education*. Abingdon: Routledge

Clarke, S (2008) *Active learning through formative assessment*. London: Hodder Education

Kelly, AV (2009) *The curriculum: theory and practice* (6th edition). London: Sage Publications

Garner, J (ed.) (2005) *Assessment and learning: theory, policy and practice*. London: Sage Publications

Marsh, C (2009) *Key concepts for understanding curriculum* (4th edition). Abingdon: Routledge

http://arrts.gtcni.org.uk/gtcni/handle/2428/4623 – 10 principles for Assessment of Learning

http://publications.teachernet.gov.uk/eOrderingDownload/Primary_curriculum_Report.pdf – Rose Review of the Primary curriculum

www.qcda.gov.uk/ and **http://curriculum.qcda.gov.uk/** – Qualifications and Curriculum Development Agency

www.ofqual.gov.uk/ – Office of the Qualifications and Examinations Regulator

www.thersa.org/projects/education/opening-minds

You can also view recent major reports on curriculum online:

www.dcsf.gov.uk/14-19/documents/Final%20Report.pdf – Tomlinson Report on 14–19 curriculum

www.education.gov.uk – New Department for Education

Chapter 4
Researching education

OBJECTIVES

By the end of this chapter you should have:
- identified appropriate criteria on which to judge the claims made by educational research;
- understood the distinctions often made between positivist and interpretative research traditions and between quantitative and qualitative data collection and analysis;
- examined some of the relationships between educational research, policy and practice;
- considered the roles of teachers and students as the subjects, interpreters and producers of research.

Introduction

In a 1996 lecture to the Teacher Training Agency, Professor David Hargreaves issued a serious challenge to all those working in the field of educational research. He suggested that publically funded research offered *poor value for money in terms of improving the quality of education provided in schools* (Hargreaves, 1996, page 1). Whereas medical practitioners effectively used medical research findings to inform their decisions, educational research did not supply a sufficient comparable evidence base for teaching. He argued that most research did not contribute to a cumulative, coherent body of knowledge and was often out of step with the interests and concerns of teachers in schools. Eight years later, in an address to the British Educational Research Association, American educational psychologist Robert Slavin drew a similar and again unflattering comparison. Slavin used the children's story of Rip van Winkle – who awoke after falling asleep for a hundred years – to emphasise what he considered to be the slow rate of progress and innovation within education as compared to other professional fields:

> If Rip had gone to sleep as a doctor at the end of the nineteenth century and woken up today, he could not simply re-enter his profession. Nor could he, as an agricultural worker, re-enter the farming industry more than a century later without considerable retraining. But after a hundred-year slumber he could, Mr Slavin suggested with a wry smile, 'make a reasonably good primary school teacher'.

> (reported in Marshall, 2004, page 36)

Like Hargreaves, Slavin blamed educational research, with its insufficient *standards of evidence*, for the relative lack of innovation in teaching practice. Both men's comments sparked considerable controversy. Both also rest upon a number of rather contentious opinions and understandings about the nature of education as well as the nature of educational research. Their criticisms do, however, reflect a more widespread and commonly expressed concern that research in education should have a significant and tangible effect on professional practice and policy-making (Hammersley, 2002). This chapter examines the impact and implications of these criticisms for contemporary educational research. It highlights the political importance given to the notion of evidence informed practice and explores the changing way that teachers have been positioned as the *subjects of, audience for* and, increasingly, *producers of research*. The chapter then critically considers the suggestion that medical research offers the most appropriate model for investigating and understanding what goes on and/or what *works well* in schools, colleges or universities. Here distinctions between positivist and interpretivist research paradigms are explained and explored. Finally, the chapter raises further important questions regarding research ethics, the political or transformatory intentions of some researchers, the agency of participants and the often neglected voices and opinions of young people within research.

The chapter is *not* intended as a 'how to' guide for those about to embark on their own educational research projects: an extensive literature in this area already exists (see for example Newby, 2010). However, it is hoped that the chapter will go some way in demystifying the research process and will encourage readers to make their own informed and critical judgements about claims made on the basis of other people's research.

Different ways of knowing: what is distinctive about educational research?

So what exactly is the function of educational research? Despite their concerns regarding the quality and relevance of much recent output, even critics like Hargreaves and Slavin clearly consider that research on educational practice and in educational settings has an important role to play in informing the decisions that educators and policymakers make. It is instructive to consider the alternatives: on what other basis could, or should, such decisions be made? The foundations of knowledge are the subject of much interesting but often rather complicated philosophical debate. For our purposes it is sufficient to highlight a number of the different ways an individual may claim to know something about education and distinguish these from knowledge informed by educational research.

Intuition is one such source of knowledge: *quick and ready insight that is not based on rational thought. To intuit is to have the feeling of immediately understanding something because of insight from an unknown inner source* (Shepard, 2010, page 35). Consider, for example, the primary teacher who may reflect, *I could just tell that he was going to be a trouble-maker so I thought I should sit him somewhere I could keep an eye on him.*

What about *tradition* and/or *common sense* as sources of knowledge? Traditional and common sense understandings are often closely related and refer to things we believe because they seem self-evident or because other people and previous generations have held them to be true. Common sense understandings may change over the years but often reflect the unexamined assumptions, preoccupations and prejudices of a particular place and time. Up until the late nineteenth century it was traditionally understood that a school-based education was inappropriate for most girls (and for working-class boys).

Even in today's classrooms, common sense understandings about the aptitudes and interests of different groups of students still endure (see for example the literature discussed in Chapters 5, 6 and 7).

Knowledge can also be imparted by *authorities* or *authoritative sources* – those who are assumed to have access to information and understanding that your average woman-on-the-street does not. In many cases, deference to the knowledge of a specialist – a doctor, car mechanic or climate change scientist, for example – is both warranted and appropriate. However, even authoritative sources can get things wrong and in some cases may even wilfully mislead or misrepresent. The credentials of those who claim or appear to be an authority may, in some cases, also be rather spurious. Ben Goldacre, of the Guardian newspaper's *Bad Science* column has famously attacked the contentions and credentials of a high-profile television nutritionist. He has also cast serious aspersions as to the pseudo-scientific claims made by the authors of the *BrainGym®* programme of, what they call, 'educational kinesiology' exercises which have been adopted in a number of British schools (see also Hyatt, 2007).

Another, very important, source of knowledge is *personal experience*. Both teachers and students learn a great deal about the inside of the educational system through spending several hours a day there for five days of a week over 40 weeks of the year. Teachers in particular acquire much of their professional knowledge on the job, learning through trial and error which techniques or schemes of work appear to be most effective in different contexts. Indeed, a common criticism of much educational research is that it ignores or undermines the expertise and practical experience of those who actually teach. Other writers, such as Lawrence Stenhouse (1985) and Donald Schön (1983) have argued that teaching should itself be conceived of as a research-based activity and emphasise that most practitioners accumulate and reflect on different forms of evidence in both deliberate and tacit ways. However, there are limits to personal experience as a source of knowledge. By definition, personal experience is restricted to unique and specific contexts – we may want to know about or understand experiences that we have not – and may never – personally experience firsthand. Moreover, the interpretations that individuals make of their firsthand experiences may be heavily influenced by intuition, alternative voices of authority and/or common sense.

SCENARIO

Imagine that you are a government minister responsible for the allocation of £280 million of public money to improve the nutritional value of school meals on the grounds that, not only would this help address rising childhood obesity, it would also result in significant improved academic achievement. On what basis would you want to make this decision? Consider the different sources of knowledge outlined above. Would these be sufficient? If not, why not? What other forms of knowledge or information might you want to be able to access?

Keep your ears and eyes open for commentary on education in the media and popular commentary (news articles, readers' letter pages, television discussion shows or radio phone-ins). On the basis of which knowledge sources are different claims about education being made?

Educational research is conducted in order to generate knowledge that is more robust, more reliable and less partisan than can be obtained from sources such as these (after Shepard, 2010, page 55). Research demands a critical assessment of information before it is accepted as accurate or true (see also Ruane, 2005). It is built upon the collection and interpretation of empirical evidence – or data – conducted in a purposeful, considered and systematic way. Belot and James (2009), for example, used research to investigate the impact of TV-chef Jamie Oliver's high-profile *Feed me Better*, improved school meals campaign. They analysed and contrasted the educational performance of primary school aged pupils in Greenwich, the first London borough to take part in the scheme, with comparable groups of pupils from schools in which the healthy meals programme had not yet been introduced. In this way they were able to conclude that improved meals appeared to increase the number of Key Stage 2 pupils who reached level 4 in English by 4.5 per cent and reduced authorised absences (likely to be related to sickness) by, on average, 15 per cent.

Bridging the gap between research and practice?

One of David Hargreaves' most pronounced criticisms was that educational research findings too seldom inform what actually happens in schools. In recent years there have been a number of programmes and interventions intended to foster a closer relationship between educational practice and educational research. As undergraduate students, you have perhaps already learned that finding the most relevant article in the right journal is a time-consuming process, and even then, the content is not always written in a language that is immediately easy to understand. The websites listed at the end of this chapter detail a number of different organisations who attempt to make research more accessible, more useful and more usable for teachers in schools. Sites such as The Department for Children, Schools and Families' Research Informed Practice Site (TRIPS), for example, or the General Teaching Council of England's Research for Teachers facility (run by the Centre for the Use of Research and Evidence in Education (CUREE)) appraise, select and summarise published research studies considered to be especially relevant for practitioners. In the case of Research for Teachers, key findings are accompanied by illustrative teacher case studies.

Another government strategy has been to encourage and support teachers to undertake their own investigation of classroom practice through practitioner or action research (for an overview of action research see Elliott, 1991). And so, for example, the recently created National Teacher Research Panel hosts a biannual conference and uses its website to offer a platform for teachers to report and discuss their own research. In extract one below, the authors describe the data collection and analysis activities conducted by a small group of primary school teachers and consider whether these can *be legitimately described as research* (Bartlett and Burton, 2006, page 395).

EXTRACT ONE

Bartlett, S. and Burton, D. (2006) 'Practitioner Research or Descriptions of Classroom Practice? A Discussion of Teachers Investigating their Classrooms'. Education Action Research, 19 (3) September 2006, pages 401–403

Three particular characteristics of action research are that it arises from practical questions, it is participatory in nature and its validity is strengthened through peer examination and discussion. The teacher researchers in this network had decided upon their individual foci based upon their own professional circumstances. They had discussed their research projects with colleagues in their schools. Thus the research was arising out of practical concerns and interests from their own place of work. It was also highly participatory in nature and involved extensive peer discussion.

Hannah and Linda had previously conducted research in their own classrooms and were now involving other teachers within their schools to see the effects of play areas and teamwork respectively. Two teachers from different schools, Julie and Sian, worked together on their research. Through the progress meetings all the teacher researchers discussed their research together and with the HE mentor and considered what data to collect and how best to collect them.

Discussions took place in these meetings about the research foci, for example different perceptions were aired concerning the benefits and issues of using teamworking with pupils. There was often a wider discussion on pedagogy. For instance, Hannah put forward her views on the significance of play across the curriculum and, with the support of others in the group, also suggested the need for this in the older age groups. This led to a discussion of constraints on the curriculum and the broader purposes of primary education.

The teacher researchers had all been involved in in-service training on pupil teams and learning strategies and so may have arrived fired up but with rather a partial view, looking for evidence to support their hopes. As noted earlier, this has been identified as a potential problem by Gorard (2002) and Foster (1999). However the network review meetings with the HE mentor as facilitator highlighted different teacher experiences, for instance of pupils working in teams. Though the teachers discussed and rationalised the differences in opinion and experiences there was a growing awareness of weaknesses and strengths in teamworking. This was further illustrated in the findings of Julie and Sian, who found teamworking to be useful in some learning situations, such as science, but far less so in others such as literacy where pupils were in ability groups and the pupil interaction and potential for teamworking were different. Similarly, Linda was very much in favour of teamworking but, after looking at it in operation in her classroom and those of other teachers in her school, had adapted it to suit different situations. This was based on her experience of when it worked best and when it was more appropriate to use other teaching and grouping strategies.

In doing the research and interacting with colleagues in the feedback sessions the teachers became more aware of the complex nature of what is often treated superficially during in-service training sessions. Alternative explanations emerged and there was also, for some, the introduction to further literature. For instance, the mentor and

Linda became involved in a discussion of the constructivist approach to learning and how Vygotsky's scaffolding concept explained certain strategies suggested in an active learning manual. She said that this theoretical explanation had given her greater insight into the learning process. Elizabeth, being very unsure and rather confused by all the different in-service training, had spent much time reading through the learning manuals and adapting them to her own strategy. She then discussed the suitability of this with the research group. This illustrates a point made by Burton and Bartlett (2005) that, as teachers become more involved in classroom research, they begin to seek out the relevant associated literature and thus often become increasingly involved in theory. It could be argued that the research process coupled with the group support and discussion had enabled these teachers to be more critical of what was presented as an officially sanctioned approach. They were able to evaluate suggested innovations and as a result to be more confident in how they developed their classroom practice.

The discussions in the research group thus show the potential of teacher research for developing the professional knowledge and understanding of those involved. Certainly being part of a network is significant if the dialogue that is a vital part of the action research process is to take place. Here we see evidence of the development of professional communities as discussed by Altrichter (2005).

Differing methods of data collection were used and varying amounts of data collected. The teachers had been unsure as to how much to collect and the advice had been to consider their working environment and teaching commitments and, in the light of these, to be practical. They did consider how data could be useful in their collection for display and in-service training purposes. Within the group a range of data were collected: photographs of pupils in the classroom, examples of pupil work, pupil accounts and interviews, interviews and comments from teacher colleagues, and personal observations of individual or small groups of children. Certainly the teacher researchers had not received any formal training in data collection and criticism can be levelled at how systematically they approached it. However, for all beginning researchers this is part of the learning process. These teacher researchers had not routinely considered the issue of validity of data collection methods. In conducting their research, though, they had in fact experienced potential for triangulation as several sources and data collection methods had usually been adopted. In some cases the research presentations demonstrated that such techniques may have been inadvertently applied rather than being part of a pre-planned strategy. However, in future research projects these teachers would be cognisant of the need to employ such validation techniques having developed an understanding of their necessity and application through experience.

It was important that the teacher researchers did not make claims that their data could not support. One constraint on how they portrayed their data, and an important characteristic of action research, was that it had to be credible with their fellow professionals. There was ongoing discussion within the research group of the methodologies used and the data collected in the regular network meetings. Final presentations to the research group were largely on PowerPoint and some also involved portfolios. The

EXTRACT ONE continued

teacher researchers explained their findings to the rest of the group and this generated real interest and questioning about what they did, how they collected data and how the data could be interpreted. Sian had also presented her findings to her staff and Linda and Hannah had discussed their research and findings with other schools' staff from the learning community on development days. This laid their findings open to further peer scrutiny which facilitated greater validation of the research process and refinement of their thinking about the findings. Over time and with suitable opportunities a number of these practitioners may develop further their interest in related literature and research findings, thus adding to their understanding of the breadth of activity that can be called research.

POINTS TO CONSIDER

- *One criticism of research undertaken by teachers is that it can be conducted from too narrow, partial and incomplete a perspective. How is – or can – this be avoided according to Bartlett and Burton's account?*

- *What are the practical and professional benefits to the participants in conducting their own research?*

- *What do you imagine might be some of the potential limitations of these teachers' research?*

What counts as 'good' educational research?

Some writers argue that to ensure reliability, educational research – whether produced by teachers or professional researchers – should adhere to certain criteria or benchmarks of good practice. In the extract above, notions of *validity*, *credibility* and *triangulation* (the use of two or more methods of data collection to explore the same phenomena) are alluded to. Certainly, if we are going to let research conclusions impact or influence the decisions we make, actions we take and, in the case of government, money we spend, we want to have a certain degree of confidence that they are not going to be completely mistaken, spurious or fabricated. However, reaching a consensus among researchers as to what constitutes good research is very difficult indeed. We might offer the expectation that good research should be: systematic, rigorous, free from bias, relevant, corroborated and/or transparent. But different researchers hold different perspectives on which of these criteria are most important and on what each term actually means. As Hodgkinson (2004, page 11) argues:

> There are almost as many different lists of suggested criteria for judging research as there are writers about the issue. These lists overlap, often substantially, but one person's obviously valid list item is judged inappropriate or excluded by someone else.

Much of the controversy that ensued after Hargreaves' comments to the TTA stem from precisely this sort of disagreement and difference in perspective.

Education research as science or art? Positivism and interpretivism

For many of the advocates of evidence informed practice, educational research should take its cue from science or, more specifically, from what is known as the scientific method whereby rigorous and methodical observation and experimentation are necessary to reveal purportedly objective truths about the world.

Measurement and the discovery of cause and effect relationships between independent variables are centrally important here. Today, this approach to research is commonly referred to as the positivist paradigm (after the *Positivist Philosophy* of French social analyst Auguste Comte). Key features most closely associated with this perspective include:

- The assumed neutrality and objectivity of a detached researcher who should attempt to minimise his or her impact upon the object of research and who is believed to be free from any bias related to social, political or cultural context.

- Data which can be quantified, that is, turned into a number, in order that statistical relationships between variables can be discerned.

- Research which is oriented towards establishing overarching patterns and trends and building theory from generalisable results.

Quantitative methods used in educational research include statistical analysis and mathematical modeling of large-scale data-sets, questionnaires, longitudinal trend surveys, behavioural or attitudinal experiments and randomised controlled trials.

This was the model of research adopted by the very first educational researchers during the late nineteenth century and it has remained heavily influential since. However, in the 1970s and 1980s, an increasing number of commentators raised serious criticisms and concerns as to the limitations of this approach. An alternative perspective was offered by those who saw research as an interpretive rather than scientific act. For these researchers, natural science is an inappropriate model for understanding education because education is a social rather than naturally occurring phenomenon not subject to the same sorts of overarching, generalisable, universal laws. Whereas the positivist tradition contends that there is one single objective reality to discover, interpretivists suggest that truth is a much more complex and slippery concept. As human beings interpret the world around them, meaning and knowledge are constructed rather than given and therefore multiple and competing interpretations of reality can coexist.

Interpretivist researchers also argue that important dimensions of social life and human experience cannot be measured in numeric or quantitative terms. And while quantitative data analysis may be good at discerning statistical relationships between different phenomena – for example, variation in the number of permanent school exclusions among students from different ethnic groups – it is not very helpful in explaining *why* such relationships exist. Interpretivist researchers are interested in exploring processes and attempt to add depth and complexity to our understandings. They use qualitative data collection and analysis, including methods such as participant observation, case study, in-depth interviewing, ethnography, photography and role play in order to try and examine people's experiences and perspectives in their own terms.

These two alternative positions can lead to quite different assumptions about what constitutes good educational research. Within the positivist paradigm, the reliability of evidence depends on the objectivity of the researcher and the methods that they use. And so, for example, in the early days of educational psychology, objective instruments to measure and compare qualities like aptitude and intelligence were developed and deployed. So long as they were asked in the exactly the same manner to each research participant, a survey list of carefully worded questions could be considered a neutral and reliable tool. From an interpretivist perspective however, positivists' claims to objectivity and neutrality are mistaken and can have damaging consequence. For interpretivists, the researcher will always have an impact upon the research they are conducting and will always approach their subject with existing assumptions, biases and ideas. Standardised instruments for measuring an individual's intelligence quotient, or IQ, for example, have been criticised as far from value free: instead of measuring general intelligence as is claimed, many of the questions used reflect cultural assumptions which privilege the western European middle class (Gould, 1981). Rather than seek to deny their inevitable biases, interpretivism suggests a researcher should attempt to critically reflect on these and make them clear. On the other hand, because qualitative studies are likely to be small-scale, critics argue that interpretivist research tends to be too idiosyncratic and of limited value in terms of generalisability or in helping to understand wider trends.

Although it is tempting to characterise interpretivism and positivism as two opposing research camps, it is not always helpful to see things in terms of a fixed either/or divide when it comes to qualitative or quantitative research (see also Pring, 2000). Interestingly, it was in fact another scientist, Stephen Jay Gould who most forcefully debunked the neutrality of IQ testing. Connolly (2007, page 4) suggests that crude, exaggerated comparisons are equivalent to *a builder arguing that hammers are better than screwdrivers. The point is that both tools are useful but for different jobs.* In extract two, Punch describes how both quantitative and qualitative methods have been used in relation to research conducted on or with children and young people in schools.

EXTRACT TWO

Punch, K (2009) An Introduction to Research Methods in Education. London: Sage, pages 46–49

As with other areas of research in social science, the historical tradition of educational and developmental psychology research was based mainly on positivism, favouring quantitative methods. The emphasis was on 'objective' and quantifiable data, with statistical analysis focusing on the aggregation of data and relationships between variables. As a result, there is a wealth of quantitatively oriented observational research on children's behavior, and multiple tests and measuring instruments exist for assessing children's developmental levels, their attitudes and their behaviours. In this research tradition, children and young people have typically been positioned passively (Veale, 2005). The emphasis has been on 'children as the objects of research rather than children as subjects, on child-related outcomes rather than child-related processes and on child variables rather than children as persons' (Green and Hogan, 2005, 2005:1). In the way child study has historically been approached, the child has also been seen as context-free, predictable and irrelevant (Hogan, 2005).

In the past two decades, however, there have been major changes in the way some research with children has been construed and approached. Sometimes called a new sociology of childhood or a new social studies of childhood, this perspective 'accords children conceptual autonomy, looking at them as the direct and primary unit of study. It focuses on children as social actors in their present lives and it examines the ways in which they influence their social circumstances as well as the ways in which they are influenced by them. It sees children as making meaning in social life through their interactions with other children as well as with adults. Finally, childhood is seen as part of society, not prior to it' (Christensen and Prout, 2005: 42). One consequence of this change has been a concern with children's perceptions, attitudes, beliefs, views and opinions. A second consequence has been a direct research focus on children's experience itself – how children interpret and negotiate their worlds, and the way in which their construction of experience shapes their perceptions and views. This approach not only seeks the child's perspective – it also acknowledges children as 'competent' human beings in their own right, rather than as 'deficient' or 'unformed' adults (Hill, 2005). They are constructed as human beings, not human 'becomings' (Qvortrup, 1987; Robert-Holmes, 2005: 55).

[. . .]

Such an approach clearly requires qualitative methods. Thus these changes are in line with the growth of qualitative methods in education research in general, and the movement of qualitative methods from the margin to the mainstream. As in other areas of education research, there has been a questioning and critique of traditional positivistic methods and of their paradigmatic and epistemological bases. This in turn has led to a broadening both of paradigm considerations and methodological approaches. In other words, positivism and post-positivism have been challenged, and other paradigms – notably interpretivism and social constructivism – have been promoted. And qualitative and ethnographic methods have become important in studies of children's experience in multiple settings. As a consequence, the methodological toolbox for research with children is now broader than it used to be, in the same way that it is for research with adolescents and adults.

[. . .]

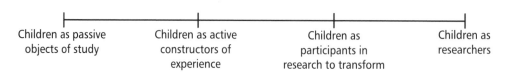

| Children as passive objects of study | Children as active constructors of experience | Children as participants in research to transform | Children as researchers |

Children in research

The greater emphasis on children's experience, together with increased recognition of their rights as citizens, has also led to a reconsideration of children's role in research. A first consequence of this is to see children as participants in research that aims at change and transformation of aspects of their lives. A second consequence, an extension of the first, is to see children as researchers themselves. The continuum (above) shows these changes in the role of children in research.

'Children as participants' in this diagram implies participatory research. In keeping with the principles of participatory research in general [. . .], participatory research with children:

- *rejects researcher-imposed realities and challenges imposed knowledge*

- *seeks ways of working with children that define their own reality*

- *promotes reciprocal learning between participants and researchers*

- *recognizes and promotes awareness of children's agency in transformations*

Research methods developed to implement these ideas are described by Veale (2005).

Even in participatory research with children, however, adults are the planners and designers. The concept of children as researchers, as in the right-hand point on the continuum (page 60), goes further, involving children in the selection of research topics, and in the shaping, planning and designing of research projects. Thus, Kellet (2005) asks why, when we place such importance on the benefits of research for the personal and professional development of adults, children should not have access to these benefits. She provides evidence, based on two years of pilot testing, that children can be taught to do empirical research without compromising its core principles. She points to a number of important learning benefits from teaching children to do research. These include the development of metacognition and critical thinking, improving the ability to develop focused research questions, extending children's logical and lateral thinking, and their organizational and management skills. Higher-order thinking is especially promoted in the data analysis stage, and research reporting and dissemination sharpens writing, communications and organizational skills. Less tangible, but equally important benefits flow from 'project ownership', particularly in terms of motivation and self-esteem. In addition to these learning benefits, there is the knowledge children can create through their own research. Kellett's book (2005) is an experience-based, step-by-step guide to teaching the research process to children aged 10–14. It also includes examples of research projects designed, executed and reported by children.

- *Think about the last time you heard about research concerning young people or children being reported in the news? Was it built on qualitative or quantitative data collection or analysis?*

- *What does Punch mean by the apparent contradiction that the child has been seen as irrelevant in much historical childhood research?*

- *Can you think of any ways in which children are presented as human 'becomings' rather than human beings in wider educational discourse?*

- *What are the benefits to children and young people in conducting their own research?*

Research ethics, agency and transformation

So far, the criteria we have considered for judging the value of educational research have concerned the quality, relevance or reliability of outputs or findings. Punch's extract suggests that we might also want to more closely consider the research *process* and not just its final results. In particular, how are individuals positioned, respected and/or impacted through their participation in the research? In the field of education, all research is expected to be conducted within a framework of ethical guidelines as outlined by the British Educational Research Association (accessible at www.bera.ac.uk/files/guidelines/ethica1.pdf). In essence, research ethics concern consideration of the informed consent of all participants (do they understand what they are taking part in and do they agree to the terms?) and the responsibility of the researcher to ensure that taking part causes participants no harm (for a much fuller discussion see www.bera.ac.uk/ethics-and-educational-research-2/).

However, some researchers take the idea of responsibility to participants further than others. In some of the literature, a third tradition or paradigm of research is identified which extends the interpretivist criticism of positivist objective neutrality and argues that researchers should be openly and actively committed to contributing *directly* to educational change (see for example, Griffiths, 1998). With regard to Punch's discussion, from this perspective it might be more appropriate to empower children and young people (as well as their teachers) to identify their own research questions and conduct their own educational research. Thompson and Gunter (2006) for example, describe their experiences of working with students-as-researchers in order to evaluate a series of policy reforms as they had been experienced at one particular secondary school. But is this compatible with the standards of evidence and push towards generalisable findings emphasised by Hargreaves and Slavin above?

SCENARIO

In a speech given to the Economic and Social Research Council in 2001, David Blunkett (then Secretary of State for Education) made the following remarks:

> One of our prime needs is to be able to measure the size of the effect of A on B. This is genuine social science and reliable answers can only be reached if the best social scientists are willing to engage in this endeavour. We are not interested in worthless correlations based on small samples from which it is impossible to draw generalisable conclusions.
>
> *(Reproduced in Hammersley, 2002, pages 83–84)*

Consider the research studies that are described or represented within this reflective reader (for example, Stephen Ball's interview-based examination of middle-class parents' decisions to send their children to specific schools (Chapter 5), Warrington and Younger's study of teachers' expectation for male and females examination success (Chapter 6) or Thompson and Gunter's high school evaluation highlighted above). Which do you think are likely to meet the key requirements for research as outlined by the British government? What do you consider their key to strengths and limitations to be?

C H A P T E R   S U M M A R Y

The chapter began by outlining the suggestion that improvements and advances in education could be made through better quality, and better use of, educational research. It described the recent commitment to evidence informed practice and outlined a number of ways in which practitioners are currently being encouraged to engage with research findings and/or conduct their own research. Some of the difficulties inherent in agreeing upon what constitutes good research in education were examined and the distinctions between positivist and interpretivist research traditions were explored.

REFERENCES

Belot, M and James, J (2009) *Healthy School Meals and Educational Outcomes.* Institute for Social and Economic Research

Connolly, P (2007) *Quantitative Data Analysis in Education. A Critical Introduction Using SPSS.* Abingdon: Routledge

Gould, SJ (1981) *The Mismeasure of Man.* New York: W.W. Norton

Hammersley, M (2002) *Educational Research, Policymaking and Practice.* London: Paul Chapman Publishing

Hargreaves, D (1996) *Teaching as a research-based profession: possibilities and prospects. Teacher Training Agency Annual Lecture.* London: Teacher Training Agency

Hodgkinson, P (2004) 'Research as a Form of Work: Expertise, Community and Methodological Objectivity'. *British Educational Research Journal* 30(1), pp9–26

Hyatt, K (2007) 'Brain Gym®: Building Stronger Brains or Wishful Thinking?' *Remedial and Special Education* 28(2), pp117–124

Marshall, M (2004) 'Bera' *Management in Education* 18(3), pp36–38

Ruane, J (2005) *Essentials of Research Methods: A Guide to Social Research.* Oxford: Blackwell

Shepard, J (2010) *Sociology.* Belmont: Wadsworth.

Schön, D (1983) *The reflective practitioner.* San Francisco, CA: Jossey-Bass

Stenhouse, L (1985) *Research as a basis for teaching.* London: Heinemann

Thomson, P and Gunter, H (2006) "From 'consulting pupils' to 'pupils as researchers': a situated case narrative". *British Educational Research Journal,* 32 (6), December 2006, pp839–856

FURTHER READING

Elliot, J (1991) *Action research for educational change.* Buckingham: Open University Press

Griffiths, M (1998) *Educational Research for Social Justice: Getting off the Fence.* Buckingham: Open University Press

Kellet, M (2005) *How to Develop Children as Researchers: A Step-by-Step Guide to Teaching the Research Process.* London: Paul Chapman

Newby, P (2010) *Research Methods for Education.* Harlow: Pearson

WEBSITES

Pring, R (2000) *The Philosophy of Educational Research*

www.standards.dfes.gov.uk/research/ – The Research Informed Practice Site (TRIPS)

www.standards.dcsf.gov.uk/ntrp/ – National Teacher Research Panel

www.gtce.org.uk/teachers/rft/ – 'Research for Teachers' (General Teaching Council for England)

www.eep.ac.uk/nerf/index.html – National Education Research Foundation

www.badscience.net/

www.education.gov.uk – New Department for Education

Theme two

Education and social justice

Chapter 5
Socio-economic class

OBJECTIVES

By the end of this chapter you should have:
- identified historical changes and continuities in the socio-economic class structure of the UK;
- considered the role performed by formal systems of education in enabling or preventing social mobility;
- recognised key characteristics of a *post-welfare society* and considered the educational implications of these.

Introduction

This chapter is concerned with inequalities and identities related to socio-economic class and emphasises the political significance of education. In extract one, a politician outlines what he sees as the crucial relationship between schooling and the idea of social mobility while extract two attempts to place political rhetoric within a wider national and international policy context. The final extract reminds us that political power is not only exercised by politicians or policy-makers. It provides a critical examination of the decisions and deliberations made by parents when considering where to send their children to secondary school.

Identity and inequalities in education

The following four chapters share a concern with issues of social justice in education. They each focus upon one particular dimension of an individual's identity and its potential impact upon their educational experience. Across these chapters, a number of recurring and interconnected arguments are emphasised.

- Identity in this context relates to the relationship between how individuals see and define themselves and how they are seen and defined by other people and by wider society.

- An individual's identity is *not* entirely determined by biology or fixed from birth. The way we see ourselves and see other people is heavily affected by processes of *socialisation* which equip and encourage us to enter into an existing framework of social relations and to perform specific social roles.

- The structure of society is such that different groups of people are positioned with different access to power and/or awarded different opportunities. There is therefore an important relationship between social identities and persistent social inequalities.

- Schools and universities are key sites for socialisation. Through formal examination systems, they also play a large part in determining the employment opportunities and income earning potential of individuals in later life. As a consequence, they offer both the potential to reproduce existing social and economic inequalities and to challenge these.

A changing picture of social class through social mobility?

The first dimension of identity we will consider is *social* - or *socio-economic* – *class*. Browne (2005, page 14) suggests that *social classes can be defined as broad groups of people who share a similar economic situation such as occupation, income and ownership of wealth.* He points out that *often these criteria are closely related to each other and to other aspects of individuals' lives such as their level of education, their status and lifestyle* as well as the level of *power and influence* they are able to exercise (2005, page 14). Gaine and George (1999) describe that:

> In the past divisions [between social classes] were more starkly visible in terms of clothing, speech, housing type and location, income and type of work. Victorian Britain had such clear divisions, with clear boundaries of wealth and status and shared assumptions about immutable differences between the classes and people's 'station in life' being fairly fixed: there were those with 'breeding' and those without ... These divisions were expressed and sustained by a distaste for social mixing, prohibitions about marriage, and a belief that the hierarchy was God-given.

They go on to argue that today the class structure looks rather different. Indeed, many commentators have suggested that the distinctions and hierarchy between supposedly upper and lower classes have become both much more flexible and much less clear. One reason for this is that Britain's economy and employment structure has changed significantly within the last 100 years. Primary industries such as coal-mining or ship-building – around which communities often described as 'working class' traditionally formed – have declined and been replaced by new, non-manual and de-territorialised service-sector industries. A further reason is that patterns of consumption and other lifestyle choices now play a much greater role: today we are likely to define ourselves as much in terms of what we buy as what we do.

Perhaps the most significant potential change stems from the promise of greater *social mobility* – that is, the opportunity for individuals to move *between* social classes rather than simply follow in the predetermined footsteps of previous generations of their family. Here, formal systems of education are seen to play a centrally important role as is reflected in extract one, a speech given by Prime Minister Gordon Brown to The Specialist Schools and Academies Trust in June, 2008.

EXTRACT ONE

Brown, G (2008) Speech to Specialist Schools and Academies Trust, *Monday 23 June. Available online at www.number10.gov.uk/Page18045*

My school motto was 'I will strive my utmost'. . . Because we lived in a mining community, the next door [school motto] . . . recalled miners coming out of the shaft into the day, and it was 'Rise to the Light', the ambition that the miners had for their own children to rise by education.

And I have looked at some of the most recently founded schools and their mottos: No goal is beyond our reach; achievement for all; aiming for excellence – all schools that are crucibles of hope, drivers of ambition, a mission for upward mobility showing that through leaders and teachers with dedication, skill and a deep belief in the value of public service, as I know you all share, the life chances of our children can be transformed.

And let us now seek therefore to build on the excellence you have achieved and let us aim to give every child in Britain a world class education to liberate the potential of all by using the most powerful weapon mankind has ever invented, and that is knowledge and its application.

Now in the last 12 months we have announced a series of reforms: the growth of one to one tuition and the importance of personal learning; the national challenge to improve low attaining schools so that every child can go to a good school; an expansion of apprenticeships and then grants for university so that every teenager has the chance of an apprenticeship or a higher education place or a place in further education; and action on the under-5s and child poverty so that every child virtually from the cradle onwards has more opportunity and no-one is left out or left behind.

And what I want to talk about today is the bigger ideas that I believe lie behind these reforms and then chart the next stage, to make good the founding idea of what I believe: it is a mission of social mobility that the next generation, whatever their background, should have the opportunity to do better than the last.

And I am interested in a new wave of social mobility, starting now, because I am a child of the first great wave of post-war social mobility. I grew up in an ordinary industrial town, I went to the local school, I benefited as I remember from great and dedicated teachers. I was fortunate enough to get to university as part of the social changes taking place at that time and I saw at first hand the power of opportunity to change lives.

But as a teenager, even then, I also saw close friends of mine who might have gone on to college or an apprenticeship or university, but who never did. University or college was they thought, or their parents thought, not for people like them. And often what were invisible barriers, the backgrounds that they came from, the assumptions they had made, the encouragement perhaps they never had, held them back to their permanent disadvantage.

[. . .]

So my own experience doesn't just lead me to celebrate the chances I had to learn to get on, to be helped when I was in trouble, they lead me to a commitment, having seen the power of opportunity to change lives and how the denial of opportunity can hold young people back, I want the opportunity to rise from the place where they are to the place where they can be, to be there for everybody. For every child we can say that their destiny is not written for them, but written by them.

[. . .]

At its core I think this is a great moral endeavour, it is a belief that everyone has some-thing to contribute, no-one should be written off before they have even had the chance. But social mobility usually starts with parents wanting their children to do better than they did themselves, but it cannot be achieved without the young people themselves adopting over time the work ethic, the learning ethic and aiming high, and it also as we know depends on schools, on education, on government giving people the capacity to participate fully in shaping their future.

Let's look back to the first big phase of post-war social mobility. It was brought about by fundamental changes in the occupational and industrial structure of the British economy, and we saw then the growth of new occupations and new professions, the rise of a sala-ried middle class and a skilled working class, a whole generation. My generation was given opportunities their parents had never dreamed of, it was the chance to become teachers and doctors and engineers and civil servants for the first time because of the 1944 Education Act, secondary education guaranteed to all. And as the children of the 50s became students in the 60s there were new grants for studies and of course new universities to study at. And this was the generation of room at the top, the children of Butler's Education Act, of Bevan's Health Service, of all the other reforms of the post-war social patriots.

But in the 1970s and 80s this rise in social mobility stalled as the restructuring of our economy took place. Remember just how many skilled manufacturing jobs were lost. As a result the opportunities for social mobility seemed to narrow, inequality and child poverty did worsen, unemployment rose to 3 million, the sons and daughters of working class families missed out on many of the new educational opportunities that were being cre-ated. And at a time when many of their fathers were being hit by unemployment, and I saw it in my own constituency in Scotland, many of the generation that some have called Thatcher's children, the lost generation, were sadly denied the chance to progress. And the result was, as detailed survey evidence has now shown, that someone born in 1970 and at secondary school in the 1980s had much less chance of moving up the social class ladder than someone born in 1958.

Now in the last 10 years we have been determined to reverse the decline. Employment has risen, investment in education has undoubtedly grown and we have made some progress. The sharp drop in social mobility has been stalled and rapid improvements in school results since the late 1990s give us a platform for a new era that can be one of accelerating social mobility.

The proportion of young people getting 5 or more GCSEs has risen by as much as a third. We have started to close the gap in achievement, thanks to many of you here, between [social] classes in both primary and secondary schools. A record 1.6 million young people aged 16 – 18 – the highest number ever – are now taking part in education, workplace learning or in training. And between 2002 and 2006, the last year for which figures are available, the gap in university participation for young people from higher and lower social and economic groups has narrowed by three and a half percentage points.

Too often and for too many decades people said there was nothing we could do to raise the performance, the skills, the ambition of the low skilled members of our community. Now everyone I think understands that with good pre-school support, with good schools and with great teachers we can make a transformational difference.

[. . .]

So the question we must address is: what will become of this generation's children? And I can tell you today I am optimistic about the prospects for the future. I believe that if we take together as a country the right long term decisions then we, Britain, can benefit from a new wave of social mobility and thus extended opportunities.

Today in Britain it is a fact that we have 6 million unskilled workers. By 2020, as a result of the changes in the global economy, a country like ours may need only half a million of these unskilled men and women. Today we have 9 million highly skilled jobs, by 2020 we will need 14 million – 5 million more – with the skills that are necessary to meet the occupational opportunities available.

And this is as fast an expansion of occupational change as we have seen in our history, a 50% rise in less than two decades in professional jobs for which we need skilled people, a 90% decline in unskilled jobs, the biggest we have ever seen.

And change may be even faster than this and opportunities may be even greater than this, because while the post-'45 wave of social mobility came from the changes wrought by the opening up of our national economy, the new wave of social mobility comes from changes that are wrought by opening up the whole global economy.

[. . .]

And in this new economic environment of global expansion and job creation, as China, India and Asia become consumers as well as producers, there will be major opportunities for those countries that are willing and able to seize these chances. And the issue therefore is not whether there will be change, change will be massive, the issue is who is going to benefit from this great transformation? How can we ensure that increased social mobility means that the benefits of change are widely shared?

And it is all the more important a question because more than ever, while the prizes for success for the individual are great, the consequences of failure are much greater still. In this new world many unskilled workers will become not only poor, but virtually unemployable. But in this new wave also there need be no ceiling on your ability to rise if you can make the effort. Indeed as the global economy expands, Britain can attract companies to Britain because of the skills that we have to offer, and if you have skills, educated in Britain, you can work almost anywhere in any part of the world.

So instead of opportunities limited by the old sheltered national economy that needed a certain number of people for particular jobs, there will be potentially unlimited opportunities for the forward march of social mobility, opened up by the changes in the wider global economy.

[. . .]

And social justice in future years may be best expressed as something more than social protection, compensating people with a safety net for what they do not have, instead it may be better expressed by social mobility, not compensating people for what they don't have, but helping people develop what they do have, their talents, their potential and their ability.

POINTS TO CONSIDER

- *Within his speech, Gordon Brown identifies a number of people whom he believes share responsibility for ensuring that the potential of every student, irrespective of class background, is fully realised. This includes teachers, parents and students themselves. What do you think teachers could do to achieve this aim? What about parents? Or students? What other people or institutions might have a role to play? Where do you think most responsibility lies?*

- *He also talks about* invisible barriers *that held some of his friends back from going on to college or university. Can you suggest what these barriers might be? What invisible, or visible, barriers to further study do you think operate today?*

- *Speaking in 2008, Brown lists a number of recent Labour party reforms in education including the growth of one-to-one tuition and expansion of apprenticeship and grant schemes. Can you think of any other recent directions taken in education policy or funding which may have compromised the promise of social mobility that Brown describes? (You may want to reflect on who Brown's audience was here).*

Obstacles to social mobility through education

Gordon Brown is by no means the first British politician to express the desire to transform Britain into a *classless society* in which *every* child's *destiny* can be written *by them* and not *for them*, and the idea that individuals can *rise by education* is a compelling one. However, education can also function to cement existing inequalities.

The very first schools and universities were private institutions intended to prepare the sons of the privileged to take up roles of future leadership. The 1870 Elementary Education Act introduced schooling *for the masses* when it became politically and economically expedient to create a workforce with basic literacy and numeracy skills. It was not until 1944's Butler Education Act and its provision of free secondary level education for all students that equality became an explicit educational pursuit. Tomlinson

(2005, page 3) writes that *the development of comprehensive education from the 1960s appeared to signal an end to education as a vehicle for the perpetuation of social class divisions and raised the hope that the talents of the whole population could be put to new social and economic use.*

Yet in March 2010, a report produced by the Organisation for Economic Cooperation and Development suggested that among more than 30 *developed world* member nations, Britain had the weakest levels of social mobility: *The chances of a child from a poor family enjoying higher wages and better education than their parents is lower in Britain than in other western countries* (Elliott 2010, online). Nunn et al. (2007, page 41) also report that, although *there continues to be substantial evidence that education is one of the most important variables influencing relative social mobility*, it would appear that *the introduction and expansion of universal education systems . . .* have not *led to increasing levels of relative social mobility* [emphasis added].

Rather than education equipping and encouraging students to *rise up* or move away from their original socio-economic background, social class continues to be *one of the key factors that determine whether a child does well in school* (Browne, 2005, page 285). Lupton, Heath and Salter (2009, page 80) describe that, in spite of small improvements in recent years, *the social class gap between the highest and lowest groups at the end of compulsory schooling is around 40 percentage points*, and while *four fifths of young people in the most advantaged 10% of areas leave schooling with five GCSEs at Grade A*-C* this is true of only two-fifths of those living in the poorest areas.

A number of competing explanations for the persistence of class-based inequalities in educational outcomes have been volunteered. Some have examined the possible material disadvantages of lower socio-economic groups (such as limited access to books, computers or other resources; home environments which are less conducive to concentrating on homework; or the necessity for some students to takeup part time jobs). Others suggest there might be cultural explanations such as different attitudes to the value of education and schools. Yet others have examined the culture of classrooms, teacher expectations and/or the focus of the curriculum to consider whether it is the education system itself which is built to reflect the interests and values of the middle classes (for an overview of these and other perspectives, see Gaine and George, 1999).

In this chapter our focus is not on the real or imagined impoverishments of working-class life or working-class families, nor on students' experiences in schools, although these issues are very important to explore. Our attention will instead remain focused on the policy decisions and priorities which impact upon both educational and wider socio-economic inequalities. A rhetorical commitment to social mobility through education is one thing, but how realistic is the promise of achievement for all in light of the existing structures and interests of the national and international economy?

Extract two is taken from a book written by educational researcher Sally Tomlinson offering a *critical overview of education policy since 1945*. She argues that during this period, *government in the UK moved from creating and sustaining a welfare state to promoting a post-welfare society dominated by private enterprise and competitive markets*. Although the book was published in 2005, Tomlinson identifies a number of tensions which may serve to undermine Gordon Brown's *mission of social mobility*.

EXTRACT TWO

Tomlinson, S (2005) Education in a Post-welfare Society [2nd edition]. Maidenhead: Open University Press, pages 220–223

Right-wing ideological beliefs in education as a mechanism for the development of an hierarchical society, in which a differentiated school and higher education system creates a stratified workforce, explains much of Conservative education policy during the twentieth century, with some acceptance of a meritocratic position. Mrs Thatcher's introduction of the Assisted Places scheme in 1980 was to 'enable talented children from poorer backgrounds to go to private schools . . . to ensure that families like my own had the chance of self-improvement' (Thatcher, 1993: 39). Influential Labour politicians, as Lawton (2005) demonstrated, had also clung to the notion of meritocracy and selection of the 'able' for a superior education, a position which in 2005 still dominated New Labour education policy. Although the Labour Party had historically also regarded education as a means to improve society in terms of social justice and equality of opportunity – demonstrated in New Labour's rhetorical commitment to social inclusion and community empowerment – explanations for current early twenty-first century policies must be linked to wider issues relating to the management of economic and social change in a global economy. New Labour policies had changed the welfare state into a competition state (Cerny and Evans, 2000, 2004), 'pushing marketisation and privatisation as zealously as the Conservatives did' (Marquand, 2004: 118) and created a society centred around consumption rather than production in which the poor could never fully participate (Bauman, 2002).

Phillip Bobbitt's (2002) polemical view of the transformation of nation states into market states goes some way towards explaining current policies, as he believes that while in the UK and the USA Thatcher and Reagan laid the groundwork for market states and 'did much to discredit the welfare rationale for the nation-state', it is Bush and Blair who 'are the first market state political leaders, offering to improve and expand the opportunities offered to the public' (Bobbitt, 2002: 222). The improvement of opportunities comes via enterprise, human capital development, tax incentives for business and meritocratic education. Market states must maximize opportunities by encouraging competition, providing incentive structures and draconian penalties – especially the threat of unemployment and loss of income – for individuals. Because multinational companies evaluate states for their workforce capabilities and other attractions for capital, market states must educate and train their populations for a global job market, but are not in the business of the redistribution of jobs or money and can no longer guarantee the welfare of all citizens. Indeed, market states are no place for mutual assistance and 'are largely indifferent to the norms of justice' (p. 230). They require more centralized government but governments can reduce the scope of their activities by handing out former responsibilities to private, charitable and other organizations. Market states encourage meritocracies where 'ruthless assessment' is the norm and any 'choices' in, for example, education, are in fact strategies in a competitive market place. Bobbitt goes further in his analysis of the endpoint of market policies in education – he envisages that 'the days of mass public education are unlikely to continue' (p.242) as various types of privatization take over. The Academies programme in England was certainly an illustration of a partial handover of state schools to privatization. Crouch had commented on all this in 2003, asking 'once public services are treated in most respects as commodities . . . how long will it be possible to defend their being subsidised and not bought or sold in the market like other commodities?' (Crouch 2003: 25).

[. . .]

The future

Predictions about the future direction of education have always proved particularly problematic, change depending on political prejudice, powerful vested interests and pressure groups. Although as Heller (1988: 24) remarked, 'politics and good intentions do not mix' New Labour's plans for education appeared replete with good intentions. Barber (2002), describing UK government strategy for education into the twenty-first century in a speech to policymakers in the USA, claimed that 'our [New Labour] vision is a world class education service'. While few would dispute the desirability of improving the education service for all, a serious question raised by the notion of global competition for world class education is 'Whose world?'

Examinations of the beneficiaries of 'high quality education', however it is defined, indicate that this kind of education has always been monopolized by higher socio-economic groups with some concession to social mobility for lower class 'gifted' individuals. The restriction of access to particular forms of education has always acted as a dominant form of social exclusion. New Labour, as with governments around the world at the end of the twentieth century, was grappling with a situation in which more and more people were engaged in a competitive attempt to gain qualifications and employment, large numbers were excluded from entering the competition in equal terms, and others, driven by heightened insecurities, were intent on retaining or gaining positional advantage. In this situation good intentions for reducing inequality and exclusion were balanced by the political reality that policies which threatened the middle and aspirant classes could threaten the government's electoral base. In addition all social groups, while told by government they had choices as consumers, increasingly felt powerless to shape their society and its institutions (Bauman, 2004). In the demolition of the welfare state, a major casualty has been the abolition of a collective voice from all those who believed that a common educational experience, equally resourced and based on shared values, was a democratic right.

One of Tomlinson's and others' central arguments is that, in spite of good intentions, a system built around competition and market forces does not lead to social equality:

The problem with New Labour education policy,[. . .] is not that it lacks a stated commitment to social justice, nor that it lacks policies. Rather, there is a problem with the depth and authenticity of its commitment because there are so many contradictions within it as well as significant silences. Social justice as redefined by New Labour has become policy to alleviate growing divisions and inequalities which the market policies embraced by the government have sustained. As Neal Lawson has pointed out, 'Social democracy will not take root in the thin social soil of competitive markets' (Lawson, 2005, page 31). Neither will selective education policies which enable some upward, but not downward, social mobility encourage a socially just, cohesive society.

(Thrupp and Tomlinson, 2005, page 552)

The politics of personal decisions

It is not the intention of this chapter to lay the blame for persistent educational inequality solely at the feet of Labour Party, nor for that matter Conservative Party, politicians (it is instructive to note that it was previous Conservative Party governments who first instigated extended periods of marketisation in education and elsewhere). Research evidence suggests that, rather than social mobility being the route to greater equality between individuals, mobility can only be realised if you first tackle social inequality: *countries with more equal incomes* [such as Denmark, Finland and Norway] *tend also to have greater differences in earnings between fathers and sons. Conversely, there is less earnings mobility in countries where income inequality is higher*, as is the case in the UK (OECD, 2008, page 7).

But tackling inequality in income means policies of redistribution of wealth and opportu-nity, and politicians believe that these are unlikely to be popular with the people who can vote them in or out of power.

A deep egalitarian version of social mobility will come up against the same political obstacles as fighting inequality in any other way. Social mobility that changes who gets the good things in life will be just as hateful to those who have them and are afraid of losing them as any other form of redistribution.

(Excell, 2009, online)

As Tomlinson has already suggested, education is an important arena in which those already in a position of advantage will do what they can to make sure that that is where they – and their families – stay. As Levitas (2005, page 17) puts it, *the middle classes will do anything to prevent their dimmer offspring from descending the social scale*. This truism has been satirised by author John O'Farrell in his novel *May Contain Nuts*. It has also been the subject of detailed examination by sociologist of education, Stephen Ball.

EXTRACT THREE

Ball, S (2006) Education Policy and Social Class: The Selected Works of Stephen J. Ball. *Abingdon: Routledge, pages 271–273*

The state sector as a risk

For some parents entrusting their children to the state sector is simply one risk that they are unwilling to take. Mrs Crichton explained, very simply, that she was 'nervous about the state sector' and the 'problem of taking a chance with your child and throwing them into the state sector'. For such parents private schools provide environments and opportunities and forms of provision which are simply not available, as they see it, to their children from the state sector. Parents like Mrs Crichton regard entering their child in the state sector as putting their child and their child's future at risk. Such a position is both moral and strategic. [. . .]. Private schools are 'class enclaves' (Teese, 2000) which offer 'long term protections from potential risk in an increasingly uncertain world' (Sedden, 2001, p. 139). As such 'the class project feels like good parenting' (Sedden, 2001, p. 139). Private schools offer a cultural milieu, 'a communicative order of self-recognition' (Teese, 1981, pp. 103–4), which is coherent and undiluted, and constitutes a 'protected enclave for class formation' (Sedden, 2001, p. 134). As Teese (2000) concludes, private schools are fortified sites within diverse school systems which represent class projects and 'renew middle class culture and collectivity in predictable ways across generations' (Sedden, 2001, p. 136). They also work to transform or reinvest economic into cultural capital. In effect these enclaves work to export risk of failure to state schools. They protect and reproduce classed 'communities of destiny'. [. . .] Private schooling limits the degree of social mixing to tolerable levels. It is a choice for exclusivity and also for advantage. It is, as Crook suggests, a basis of solidarity, in effect, of 'recognition'. In a sense, it is an enclave in which neo-liberal policies do not operate. The risks threatened by equality through choice can be avoided. And indeed, for some families the private sector has an obviousness to it. It is a non-choice. It is 'an alternative to constant "choice", anxiety and isolation' (Crook, p. 181) and mobilises 'versions of safety and certainty' (p. 182). Choice of private school avoids the 'chronic problematization of the signifier' (Lash, 1994, p. 157) that attends the question of what is a 'good' state school. The private schools are 'instead rooted in shared meanings and routine background practices' (Lash, 1994, p. 159). [. . .]

> Everyone I know either went to a grammar school or a private school . . . so it's something . . . comprehensive to me is a complete unknown quantity, so therefore it's alarming, only based on ignorance really. And also you do have to handle those . . . varying degrees, you are not in an environment where everybody wants to work.

Here Mrs Grafton is willing to take the risk of sending her child to state school but she does this reflexively and her language of 'panic' and 'alarm' gives some indication of the emotional underpinnings of the decision-making involved. Rational and affective responses are messily mixed. For Mrs Grafton the comprehensive school is an unknown, and she is anticipating difficulties in 'an environment' where not 'everyone wants to work'. The 'not everyone' is the 'other', those children who are not like mine. These are the risks of social mix, of boundary crossing, of going outside of grid and group (Pakulsi and Waters, 1996, p. 118). Indeed, Douglas suggests that risk works to maintain cultural boundaries (Lupton, 1999, p. 4). Risk is a response to the unknown, the dangerous. It can make us cautious, inward-looking. In the case of schooling, these are risks that have to be managed, 'handled' by the family.

[. . .]

Anxiety, emotion and class choosing

Obviously, we see various capitals intertwined here. There is an emotional as well as social and material expenditure involved in choice-making. While I do not want to overplay the emotional and psychological aspects of the market behaviour of parents and students, there are constant worries about getting things wrong, about failing the child, about mis-taking priorities, about not finding the perfect school or right university; 'the extent of parents' ethical and social responsibility today . . . is historically unprecedented . . . The contemporary family is under a pressure to educate' (Beck Gersheim, 1996, page 143). The other side of all this is various forms of guilt. Both a personal guilt about letting the child down or in some cases social guilt about choosing private schooling in preference to the state sector (see Ball, 2003c). As one parent put it simply, you make judgements about yourself (Mrs Cornwell).

[. . .] Parents, in part, become middle-class moral subjects by learning and acquiring behaviours and attitudes from others in their class setting. In this anxiety can be con-tagious but panic is offset by deliberation, emotion by rationality: we don't just make judgements, we worry, sometimes agonise, about them . . . (Kymlicka, 1989, page 11).

POINTS TO CONSIDER

- *Ball argues that private schools work to transform or reinvest economic into cultural capital. Can you suggest what he might mean by this?*

- *Choice in education provision is often presented as a good thing in political discourse. How is it characterised here?*

- *Reflect on the choices that your parents made concerning your education and/or the choices you have made, or may make, for children of your own. Under what circumstances may those decisions have been made differently?*

Ball's research reminds us that social class is not just about questions of income or job-type. Later in the same article he suggests that there is a *lived reality of class* which has an *emotional* dimension and which involves *gut feelings* about which other people are *people like us* and in which places or situations we feel *at home* (see also Reay 2005). The extract also shows us that private, personal decisions contribute to political relationships of power.

C H A P T E R   S U M M A R Y

This chapter has shown that there is a complex relationship between education, politics and social inequality. It has characterised the current policy context as one in which competition, choice and increasing marketisation may serve to undermine education's potential to lead to greater social mobility. The chapter suggested that class-based identities and inequalities are clearly impacted upon by policy decisions taken at the level of national government but are also enacted through choices made by individuals and families in their day-to-day lives.

REFERENCES

Browne, F (2005) *An Introduction to sociology*. Cambridge: Polity Press

Elliott, L (2010) 'OECD: UK has worse social mobility record than other developed countries'. *The Guardian* [online] 10 March 2010 **www.guardian.co.uk/business/2010/mar/10/oecd-uk-worst-social-mobility**

Excell, R (2009) 'The politics of social mobility' *Touchstone* (TUC) 13 January **www.touchstoneblog.org.uk/2009/01/the-politics-of-social-mobility/**

Gaine, C and George, R (1999) *Gender, 'race' and class in schooling: a new introduction*. London: RoutledgeFalmer

Levitas, R (2005) *The imaginary reconstitution of society, or, why sociologists and others should take utopia more seriously*. Inaugural Lecture, University of Bristol, 24 October, Available at: **www.bristol.ac.uk/sociology/staff/inaugural.doc**

Lupton, R, Heath, N. and Salter, E. (2009) 'Education: New Labour's top priority' in J. Hills, T Sefton and K Stewart (eds.) *Towards a more equal society? Poverty, inequality and policy since 1997*, Bristol: Policy Press

Nunn, A, Johnson, S, Monro, S, Bickerstaffe, T and Kelsey, S (2007) *19 Factors influencing social mobility*, Research Report No. 450, London: Department of Work and Pensions

OECD (2008) *Growing Unequal? Income Distribution and Poverty in OECD Countries.* OECD Publishing

Thrupp, M and Tomlinson, S (2005), 'Introduction: Education policy, social justice and "complex hope"' *British Educational Research Journal* 31(5), pp549-556

FURTHER READING

O'Farrell, John (2005) *May Contain Nuts*. London: Doubleday

Reay, D (2005) '"Unruly places": Inner-city comprehensives, middle-class imaginaries and working-class children' *Urban Studies* 44(7), pages 1191–1201.

Chapter 6
Gender

Introduction

In little over one hundred years the position of women and girls in society has, in many respects, been dramatically transformed and several significant changes have taken place within just the last few decades. As Murray (2009, online) reminds us:

> A girl born in 1899 [. . .] had little chance of evading the role that was considered her destiny – to marry young, stay home and raise a family. Her forebears in the late nineteenth century had struggled hard to improve her chances of an education [. . .] Yet still, only the privileged few, whose fathers or husbands were enlightened enough to permit it, got a foot on the ladder of opportunity.

Women at the turn of the century were denied the right to vote in elections, were barred from entering professions such as accountancy and the law and were unable to initiate divorce proceedings on the same grounds as men. Their status, in legal, political, social and economic terms, was widely assumed to be subordinate to that of their fathers, brothers or husbands. Right up until 1975, with the passing of the Sex Discrimination Act and enactment of the 1970 Equal Pay Act, employers could legally pay women lower salaries than male colleagues performing the same role and banks could refuse a woman a mortgage if she was unable to provide the signature of a male guarantor.

This chapter offers an introduction to a body of literature and argument known as gender theory which has been used to describe, explain and ultimately challenge the historical domination of women by men. It suggests that these theoretical understandings might be useful if we want to critically examine potential relationships between gendered inequalities and schools. The chapter then considers the argument that, after four decades of increasing equal rights and anti-discrimination intervention in education, *the gender seesaw* [has] *tipped too far*, and attention should now be focused on the relative academic underachievement of boys (Holland, 1998, page 174).

Understanding gender theory

The notion that there is a single collection of ideas that we could label gender theory is in fact a little misleading. Different writers offer rather different perspectives and gender is the subject of much complex and often rather abstract discussion and debate. However, one centrally important argument is often shared: that supposedly commonsense understandings and assumptions about the differences between men and women, or boys and girls, should be approached with suspicion and critically scrutinised. In the extract below, Sandra Lipsitz Bem, an American psychologist, uses the metaphor of *lenses* to suggest that the manner in which we are encouraged to think about males and females has been filtered or distorted in a number of powerful, but often hidden (or unexamined) ways.

EXTRACT ONE

Bem, SL (1993) The Lenses of Gender: Transforming the Debate of Sexual Inequality. London: Yale University Press, pages 1–3

Throughout the history of Western culture, three beliefs about women and men have prevailed: that they have fundamentally different psychological and sexual natures, that men are inherently the dominant or superior sex, and that both male-female difference and male dominance are natural. Until the mid-nineteenth century, this naturalness was typically conceived in religious terms, as part of God's grand creation. Since then, it has typically been conceived in scientific terms, as part of biology's – or evolution's – grand creation.

[. . .]

As profound as the transformation of America's consciousness has been during the past 150 years, hidden assumptions about sex and gender remain embedded in cultural discourses, social institutions, and individual psyches that invisibly and systemically reproduce male power in generation after generation. I call these assumptions the lenses of gender. Not only do these lenses shape how people perceive, conceive, and discuss social reality, but because they are embedded in social institutions, they also shape the more material things – like unequal pay and inadequate day care – that constitute social reality itself.

The purpose of this book is to render those lenses visible rather than invisible, to enable us to look at the culture's gender lenses rather than through them, for it is only when Americans apprehend the more subtle and systemic ways in which the culture reproduces male power that they will finally comprehend the unfinished business of the feminist agenda.

The first lens embedded in cultural discourses, social institutions, and individual psyches is the lens of androcentrism, or male-centredness. This is not just the historically crude perception that men are inherently superior to women but a more treacherous underpinning of that perception: a definition of males and male experience as a neutral standard or norm, and females and female experience as sex-specific deviation from that norm. It is thus not that man is treated as superior and woman as inferior but man is treated as human and woman as 'other.'

The second lens is the lens of gender polarization. *Once again, this is not just the historically crude perception that women and men are fundamentally different from one another but the more subtle and insidious use of that perceived difference as an organizing principle for the social life of the culture. It is thus not simply that women and men are seen to be different but that this male-female difference is superimposed on so many aspects of the social world that a cultural connection is thereby forged between sex and virtually every other aspect of human experience, including modes of dress and social roles and even ways of expressing emotion and experiencing sexual desire.*

Finally, the third lens is the lens of biological essentialism, *which rationalizes and legitimizes both other lenses by treating them as the natural and inevitable consequences of the intrinsic biological natures of women and men. This is the lens that has secularized God's grand creation by substituting its scientific equivalent: evolution's grand creation. As we shall see, nothing in this book denies biological facts, but I do argue that these facts have no fixed meaning independent of the way that a culture interprets and uses them, nor any social implications independent of their historical and contemporary context.*

The lenses of androcentrism, gender polarization, and biological essentialism systemically reproduce male power in two ways. First, the discourses and social institutions in which they are embedded automatically channel females and males into different and unequal life situations. Second, during enculturation, the individual gradually internalizes the cultural lenses and thereby becomes motivated to construct an identity that is consistent with them.

- *Bem is writing primarily about American culture and society at the close of the twentieth century. Can you identify any similarities or differences here with ideas about men and women in other places and/or times?*

- *In the introduction of this chapter we suggested that over the last century the position of women and girls in society has been significantly transformed. To what extent do you think each of Bem's lenses of gender still apply?*

- *Bem suggests that gender lenses are embedded in social institutions. This would include schools and universities. Can you think of any examples of how androcentrism, gender polarisation or biological essentialism could be reflected in either universities or schools?*

Gender as a social construction

Bem argues that people's *ideas* about differences between the sexes are really important: *not only do lenses shape how people perceive, conceive and discuss social reality [. . .] they also shape the more material things, that constitute social reality itself.* For example, if females are characterised as 'naturally' more emotional, irrational or immature than males, it is all the more easy and convincing to argue that it is in everyone's best interest if they are not allowed to work as lawyers or to vote. And, as we shall see in a later extract, if a teacher automatically assumes that boys are more academically able in certain subjects, say mathematics or science, this can result in fewer female students being entered for these qualifications at an advanced level, ultimately leading to fewer women mathematicians and scientists.

Carrie Paechter (1998, page 38) writes, *when a child is born, we want to know immediately if it is a boy or a girl.* Consider this for a moment, why do you think that this is so? She continues:

> *The way we react to this information is based on a whole set of social and cultural assumptions about that individual's gendered future. Although gender is usually ascribed to babies on the basis of perceived anatomical distinctions, our assumptions about the child's future are more to do with social and cultural values than with the direct consequences of such bodily features; we assume, however that these cultural differences will follow fairly automatically from the physical ones.*

The crucial point in both Paechter's and Bem's argument is that we must distinguish between biological sex – the physical body that an individual is born with, for most people either *male* or *female* – and gender – the socially constructed expectations for male and female behaviour characterised as *masculinity* and *femininity*. Ann Oakley emphasises this same point when she describes how anthropologists have shown that, far from being inevitable or biologically determined, what it means to act like a man or behave like a woman varies considerably in different cultural contexts and over time (Oakley, 2005).

The power and consequence of binary thought

Paechter, Bem and Oakley additionally argue that it is important to recognise that, in Western cultures, masculinity and femininity are constructed not just as different from each other but as mutually exclusive opposites. If you are one thing, you are not the other: acting like a man (or boy) is defined in close relation to *not* acting like a woman or girl. In this way, the many important similarities between individuals of different sexes are undermined or ignored, as are the multiple differences that exist *among* those identified as male or female.

Gender theorists claim that this kind of binary thinking (in terms of *either/or*) is a centrally important – but potentially very damaging – feature of Western philosophy. Other deep-rooted oppositions include: mind *versus* body, reason *versus* emotion, public *versus* private (or civic *versus* domestic), action *versus* passivity, domination *versus* subordination, science *versus* nature. Paechter argues that, in each case, one term tends to be valued over the other in the popular imagination.

> *One of the most important of these dichotomies is man/woman. The other pairs are then lined up beneath them, with all the positive attributes on the male side (Lloyd and Duveen, 1992). Thus for example, Western philosophy values reason (seen as male) over emotion (female) (Connell, 1995), and sets great store by the ability of the mind (male) to transcend the body (female) (Spelman, 1982). In a discourse in which everything is either/or, then to be male is to be rational, concerned with the mind and active in civil society, while to be female is to be emotional, concerned with the body and passively waiting at home.*

(Paechter, 1998, page 8)

Paechter suggests that this is why girls and women were initially completely excluded from formal systems of education. Schools and universities were institutions in which reason should be exercised over emotion in order to equip individuals to take part in active civic life. Girls were positioned outside of this discourse. Some nineteenth-century commentators even expressed concern that over-educated women would compromise and endanger their femininity and may even become infertile or unable to breastfeed.

Girls' education in the late nineteenth and twentieth century

Greater opportunities for female education resulted from the 1870 Education Act which established a system of mass state schooling for *all* children between the ages of five and ten. However, this system was itself heavily inscribed by androcentric (or male-centred) values and, for many years, girls were educated primarily *for their future domestic roles* (Skelton and Francis, 2009, page 4). Throughout the twentieth century, the education system adapted – albeit sometimes rather reluctantly – in response to wider social, economic and political change. However, powerful gender stereotypes continued to operate in British classrooms and curriculum materials for several decades. At a policy level, the Norwood, Crowther and Newsome reports of 1943, 1959 and 1963 respectively, each to a greater or lesser extent reflected the concern that schools should help to equip male and female pupils to perform different, gendered roles (Gaine and George, 1999; Skelton and Francis, 2009).

In Britain, and across much of the Western world, the so-called sexual revolution and powerfully active women's liberation and feminist movements of the 1960s and 1970s encouraged educators and educational researchers to focus attention on the part played by the education system in perpetuating wider gender inequality. Feminist teachers began to collect evidence and report on unequal school staffing patterns, gender stereotyping in teaching texts and the limited choices made by female students in terms of future career path and subject choice (Weiner, 1994). Researchers critically examined and documented the ways in which male students commonly monopolised classroom environments and how interactions between staff and students helped to socialise girls into subservient and submissive roles (Kelly, 1986).

Gender and education today

However, over the last two decades, the discourses concerning gender issues in education have significantly changed. Partly in response to the growing importance of competitive market forces, in recent years, public and political concern with schooling has increasingly been focused on the performance of different groups of students in standardised tests and examinations such as GCSEs. Unfortunately, these statistics have not always been very carefully interpreted or accurately reported. And while some very important issues of apparent inequality have been brought to wider attention, others have been exaggerated or oversimplified.

Extract two is taken from a publication commissioned by the Department for Children, Schools and Families in order to highlight what the authors regard to be common current myths and misperceptions concerning gender issues in schools. They also attempt to suggest the reality behind each myth with reference to recent findings from educational research.

EXTRACT TWO

DCSF (2009) Gender and Education: Mythbusters. *Nottingham: DCSF Publications, pages 3–7*

Myth: All boys underachieve, and all girls now achieve well at school.

Reality: Many boys achieve highly, and conversely many girls underperform.

Analysis of the attainment data shows that other factors or a combination of factors, such as ethnicity and social class, have a greater bearing on educational achievement than gender considered on its own. Planning to address underachievement needs to take this potential interrelationship into account. Schools need to consider the relative impact of gender, ethnicity and social class in their particular setting and analyse their performance data in this light.

(Sources of evidence: DfES (2007))

Myth: Boys underachieve across the curriculum.

Reality: Boys broadly match girls in achievement at maths and science.

Boys outperform girls in maths at Key Stage 2, and continue to outnumber girls at higher level maths. But there is a large gender gap favouring girls in English. This pattern is broadly reflected across OECD nations, and is of long-standing. (In the1950s and 60s it was commonplace to explain this difference in terms of boys' late development in language and literacy skills. Such relatively poor performance was not expected to hinder their educational progress over the long term.) Early diagnosis and intervention through structured support for literacy skills as part of the early years foundation stage and primary curriculum is likely to be particularly important. Whilst the gender gap in attainment for English is relatively constant across social groups, schools with poor English performance may well find that both boys and girls are underachieving.

(Sources of evidence: DfES (2007))

Myth: Boys' educational performance suffers because the existing school curriculum doesn't meet boys' interests.

Reality: There is no evidence to suggest that the content of the secondary curriculum reflects particularly gendered interests, or that such interests equate with attainment.

It is true that since the 1980s girls as a group have performed much better in science and maths subjects, and are now more likely to stay on to further and higher education. The main reasons for this are girls having equal access to the curriculum and the end to subject specialisation at 14 with the introduction of the National Curriculum; together with changes in the employment market so that most girls envisage a 'career' once they leave school. However, girls remain underrepresented in STEM [science, technology, engineering and maths] subjects at university and the introduction of the new 14-19 diploma route means that, unless schools provide active guidance, both boys and girls may once again 'opt' for gender-stereotyped education routes at 14.

(Sources of evidence: Arnot, David and Weiner (1999), Francis (2000), Moss (2007))

Myth: Boys are 'naturally' different to girls, and learn in different ways.

Reality: There is little evidence to suggest that neurological ('brainsex') differences result in boys having different abilities/ways of learning to girls.

Recorded patterns of difference are slight, and widely debated. Neurological research remains in its infancy, and even proponents of neurological gender difference caution that there is more within sex difference in abilities than between *sex difference, meaning that teaching boys and/or girls as though these are discrete groups will fail to meet the needs of many boys and girls.*

(Sources of evidence: Baron-Cohen (2004), Slavin (1994))

Myth: Boys and girls have different learning styles, which teaching needs to match.

Reality: Learning styles as a concept are highly contested. There is no evidence that learning styles can be clearly distinguished one from another, or that these learning styles are gender specific.

In spite of the widely-held belief that boys and girls tend to have different learning styles, there is little evidence to bear this out. Research has questioned the validity of notions of discrete learning styles, and studies have also failed to find conclusive links between gender and learning style. Where learning practices and preferences may be gendered (for example, girls enjoying group work etc), such preferences may be due to social norms, suggesting a role for teachers in broadening (rather than narrowing) learning approaches.

(Sources of evidence: Coffield et al. (2004), Younger et al. (2005)).

Myth: Coursework favours girls and 'sudden death' examinations favour boys.

Reality: Changes in assessment practice reducing the value of the GCSE coursework component have had little impact on gendered achievement patterns.

Girls' results were improving prior to the introduction of the GCSE assessment model. Changes in the 1990s reducing the GCSE coursework component had little impact on gender achievement patterns. As a group girls appear to do well at sudden death examinations and coursework assessment.

(Sources of evidence: Arnot et al. (1999), Bleach (1998), Elwood (2005))

Myth: Boys prefer male teachers.

Reality: For the majority of boys and girls, the teacher's gender has no bearing on their preferences for a teacher.

Whilst males are under-represented at all phases of schooling, studies have shown that the vast majority of boys and girls prioritise a teacher's individual ability as a teacher, and their level of care for their students, rather than a teacher's gender. There have also been many studies investigating potential correlations between teacher gender and pupil achievement, and most of these have found no relationship between matched pupil-teacher gender and pupil achievement. Further, evidence does not suggest that teaching approaches or attitudes differ according to teacher gender.

(Sources of evidence: Ehrenberg et al. (1995), Lahelma (2000), Skelton et al. (2009), Francis et al. (2008a; 2008b), Carrington et al. (2007, 2008), Skelton (forthcoming)).

Myth: Boys benefit from a competitive learning environment.

Reality: Competitive learning practices may actively disengage those boys who do not immediately succeed.

Social constructions of gender encourage boys to be competitive. However, such constructions also involve a dislike and/or fear of 'losing'. Given there can only be a few 'winners' in competitive educational practices, those boys failing to 'win' academically may disengage, or find alternative ways of 'winning', for example by becoming disruptive. The current pattern of boys' attainment, with a longer tail of underachievement developing behind those boys who are high achievers, suggest that the difficulties lie with motivating those who do not immediately succeed in order that they may engage with purposeful learning.

(Sources of evidence: Jackson (2002; 2006), Elkjaer (1992))

[. . .]

Myth: Changing or designing the curriculum to be 'boy-friendly' will increase boys' motivation and aid their achievement.

Reality: Designing a 'boy-friendly' curriculum has not been shown to improve boys' achievement.

There is no evidence to show that where schools have designed or changed parts of their curriculum to be more appealing to boys ('boy-friendly') that it improves boys' achievement. Such changes may involve gender-stereotyping which can lead teachers to ignore pupils' actual preferences and limit the choices that either boys or girls can make. Schools where boys and girls achieve highly, with little or no gender gaps in subjects (particularly English), have high expectations of all pupils; have not designed a 'boy-friendly' curriculum; and in English encourage all pupils to read widely, offer them plenty of choices and plan to both engage children's interests and extend the range of reading.

(Sources of evidence: Pickering (1997), Lingard et al. (2002; 2003),
Keddie and Mills (2008), Younger and Warrington et al. (2005))

Myth: Girls are naturally better at reading and writing.

Reality: Girls in general do perform better than boys at English, and the gap between boys' and girls' performance at Key Stage 2 is much larger in writing than reading. However, the largest gaps in English performance are at school level.

The reasons why there is unequal performance in English amongst pupils and between schools are complex. Attempts to explain why high-performing schools with little gender gap in their performance do so well have found no evidence that they tailor their reading curriculum to boys' interests, or champion 'boy-friendly' pedagogies. Rather, they have high expectations of both boys and girls in English; provide a high quality and inclusive English curriculum; and are very successful both in teaching the basic skills involved in learning to read and write, and in providing extensive opportunities for children to use and extend the skills they have developed in rewarding ways.

(Sources of Evidence: DfES (2007); Younger and Warrington et al. (2005);
Moss (2007))

As Skelton and Francis note, and as is reflected throughout extract two, *from the mid-1990s onwards, the 'problems of educating boys' have dominated government agendas on educational policy and grabbed media headlines in the UK* (2009, page 103). Comparisons of male and female students' performance in National Curriculum assessments and GCSEs consistently suggest that girls are doing better than boys. For example, in 2009 in England, 54.4 per cent of girls achieved 5 or more A*-C grade GCSEs or equivalent including English and mathematics compared to 47.1 per cent of boys (DCSF 2010).

Certainly, this persistent gendered gap in academic achievement is important to address and in recent years *acres* of research and commentary has been produced in an attempt to do just that (Skelton and Francis, 2009, page 103). But are newspaper headlines which warn that, *Boys are being failed by our schools* (Clark, 2006) as *girls have forged even further ahead in the GCSE battle of the sexes* (Clark and Harris, 2002) helpful to our understanding here? And how useful are appeals to make the curriculum more *boy-friendly* and schools *less feminised*? (Clark, 2006).

It could be argued that the recent framing of boys' underachievement – and in particular, many of the proposed solutions – illustrate Bem's gender lenses at work. Warrington and Younger, for example, argue that the attention given to boys' educational underachievement is disproportionate and reflects society's wider androcentric concerns: *The gaze of the media and the preoccupation of government with issues of male achievement ought not to surprise us, since the whole structure and ethos of the English educational system have enshrined a preoccupation with boys* (2007, page 223).

The polarisation of male and female gendered identities and claims made on the basis of supposedly natural or inherent differences between the sexes are also apparent. By presenting the situation in schools as a *battle of the sexes* for exam success, and by constantly framing the argument in terms of boys' needs *as opposed to* girls', differences *among* boys and *among* girls are often neglected or ignored. There is also scant recognition that *both* boys' and girls' exam success have improved in recent years. Moreover, many of the explanations offered and/or solutions proposed to address the gender gap rest upon – and could serve to reinforce – rather crude assumptions about gender identities and norms. What does it mean to make a curriculum more *boy-friendly*, for example? Friendly to which boys? As the authors of extract two suggest, narrow conceptions of boys' interests and stereotyped expectations of masculine behaviour can actually be part of the problem for many boys in schools (see also Connolly, 2004).

One further consequence of the overwhelming shift in focus to boys' educational undera-chievement is the assumption that the issues of concern which motivated feminist activism and research in the 1970s and 1980s have been resolved. Extract three is taken from a journal article published in 2000, in which the authors argue strongly that this is not the case. Using data collected in 20 English secondary schools, they suggest that girls *continue* to encounter a number of gendered obstacles during their school careers, not least in terms of teachers' expectations as detailed below.

EXTRACT THREE

Warrington, M and Younger, M (2000) 'The Other Side of the Gender Gap' Gender and Education 12(4), pages 503–506

A further aspect of concern over girls' experiences was apparent when GCSE entry patterns in some (but not all) schools were analysed. In 1995–96 in school S2, for example, in a year when otherwise there was little evidence of a gendered pattern of entry, and more girls achieved 5 A*–C grades at GCSE than boys, a much higher proportion of boys than girls entered for all three single sciences. Table I clearly shows that the entry pattern for science gave boys greater opportunity to achieve five or more GCSE passes at grade C or above. Equally, however, the data in Table II show additional discrimination against girls, mirroring teacher perception and expectation; of the highest achieving students in the school, only 8% of boys were not entered for the three single sciences, compared to a remarkable 33% of girls; less stark but still significant is the entry pattern for the lower achieving students in the school, again favouring the boys.

Table I: Pattern of GCSE science entries in school S2 (1995/96)

	Entered for all 3 single sciences (%)	Entered for dual sciences (dual award) (%)	Entered for single science (one award only) (%)
Boys	48	47	5
Girls	27	63	10

Table II: Pattern of GCSE results in school S2 (1995/96)

	% students who achieved at least 5 A/A* awards (highest achievers in school) and were not entered for three single sciences	% students who achieved 7 GCSE awards, mostly at grade C (lowest achievers in school) and were entered for three single sciences
Boys	8	13
Girls	33	8

This entry pattern reflects continuing anti-girls discrimination in science in this particular school, evident each year since the early 1990s, but it is a pattern which a new headteacher and a new head of science were seeking, with some success, to redress. The pattern is mirrored, albeit to a lesser degree, in two of the other three selective schools, and there must be a clear concern that only very able girls are encouraged to enter for the three single sciences, whilst more relatively less able boys are entered for the separate sciences; such an entry pattern does restrict opportunities for girls, the more so when, in at least two of these schools, dual entry science is seen as a less than adequate preparation for A level study of a science subject.

[. . .]

These uneven expectations are further evident when a comparison is made of teachers' predictions of GCSE results with actual outcomes in comprehensive schools (1996) and selective schools (1997) (see Table IV). Whilst there is clear evidence of underprediction by teachers, particularly in the selective schools, of boys in English and girls in science, there is little evidence of a significant gendered pattern of underprediction. At the other extreme, however, it is clear that in both types of schools, in the subjects analysed, teachers overpredicted greater proportions of boys than girls; except in English, teachers' normal expectations appeared to be that at least 20% of the boys would achieve higher grades than they actually did. It appears that it is their teachers, as well as boys themselves, who expect boys to achieve high grades despite the lack of sustained effort and tangible achievement during their GCSE courses.

Table IV: Comparison of teacher predictions and actual GCSE results

Sex and subject	No. of predictions		Students under predicted by 1 or more grade %		Students over predicted by 1 or more grade %	
	C	S	C	S	C	S
Girls: English	109	46	27	24	12	2
Girls: Science	127	75	19	47	17	7
Girls: Geography	56	30	24	23	20	20
Boys: English	117	55	26	58	21	2
Boys: Science	139	103	16	23	24	20
Boys: Geography	70	41	22	32	25	29

C = comprehensive schools; S = selective schools

Such perceptions were spontaneously introduced into the interviews by 50% of the teachers in the comprehensive schools, and 62% of selective school teachers. In these interviews, it was often very apparent that, despite the fact that they praised girls for their conscientious, committed and mature approach to their work, many preferred to teach boys, found them more interesting than girls, and were prepared to give more time and attention to motivating and engaging boys in on-task activity (Gordon, 1996). These teachers perceived boys to be livelier in discussion, more willing to voice opinions than girls, and sharper on the uptake. Despite the contrary evidence provided by girls' work rate and attitudes, the quality of girls' written work and examination performances, boys appeared to be more valued, possessing some 'kind of potential that leads to brilliance, even if their current classroom performance exhibited no tangible evidence of it' (Walkerdine, 1994). Thus, a substantial number of teachers continued to perpetuate and to sustain what Cohen (1996, p. 133) has called 'the fiction of boys' potential':

> *Boys aren't as good at completing all the written work, but any sort of scientific work, they can cope much better than the girls. Boys frequently present more original work, whereas girls copy sentences from textbooks, write much more, take a greater pride in their work. (male teacher, C3)*

In some schools, there was a suggestion, frequently voiced by senior male staff, that boys had some sort of intuitive capacity which gave them the potential to achieve better than the girls, if only they devoted themselves to the work. But this failure to apply themselves and the resultant perceived underachievement, was rarely condemned; rather, there was at times a concealed admiration for these boys, a sense of alliance with them, almost pride in the high ability underachieving boy who at times pulled it off and achieved high grades seemingly without effort. The view, expressed succinctly by a female head of department, summarised the sentiments of many:

> *When I taught a bright all-girl group, they were committed, quiet, they all got on, left me feeling a bit of a spare part at times. I wanted a bit more sparkle and challenge; girls are more consistent, more middle of the road, less bragging, very often unwilling to dare, and to take risks. (C3)*

Such a view was quite commonplace; indeed, in a wide-ranging set of interviews, only one teacher expressed an alternative view:

> *Having classes that have been dominated by girls has been a breath of fresh air, because they appear totally committed to their end product, and I don't think I've ever had to say, 'come on, you are not on task'. It has been a bit of an eye opener really. (male head of year, C3)*

There was, then, a paradox in teachers' attitudes and approaches to girls and boys; as Kruse has pointed out:

> *Although teachers often have problems controlling boys' behaviour, they usually have a positive view of boys. But teachers, female as well as male, are often ambivalent in their opinions of girls. (Kruse, 1996, p.178)*

At its extreme, this ambivalence was expressed in terms of apology about the high achievements of girls and sympathy for the plight of boys as they struggled to cope with emancipated women and very successful girls who made them feel inadequate! In the words of a female head of department:

> *I have to say that I feel genuinely sorry for the boys: it is expected that they achieve and perform, and in terms of relationships they have to be quite up front. The girls often look as though they have got the whole thing cracked, but they can have a quiet weep and feel much better. It is not acceptable for boys to do that. I really wouldn't come back as a man. I think they have so many things to face, so many demands made of them. (C2)*

- *Can you identify any connections between this article and the gender theory perspectives outlined above? For example, what appear to be the characteristics that teachers most commonly attribute to their male and female students?*

- *The research for this article was conducted in 1997. How do you think the picture that emerges of classroom practice and teacher expectation relates to schools today?*

- *Do you have any thoughts or suggestions on how these issues could be addressed?*

C H A P T E R   S U M M A R Y

This chapter has suggested that insights from the wider field of gender theory can instructively be used to examine the different experiences of boys and girls at school. In particular, the chapter has argued that gender identities should be understood and approached as social constructions and that supposedly commonsense assumptions about natural or inevitable differences between boys and girls or men and women should be treated with caution and critically explored.

REFERENCES

Clark, L (2006) 'Boys are being failed by our schools' *The Daily Mail* [online] 13 June 2006. **www.dailymail.co.uk/news/article-390319/Boys-failed-schools.html**

Clark, L and Harris, S (2002) 'The boys are left standing as the GCSE gender gap grows' *The Daily Mail* [online] **www.dailymail.co.uk/news/article-134604/The-boys-left-standing-GCSE-gender-gap-grows.html**

DCSF (2010) *Key Stage 4 Attainment by Pupil Characteristics: Statistical First Release*. [online] 4 March 2009. **www.dcsf.gov.uk/rsgateway/DB/SFR/s000900/SFR34_2009Revised.pdf**

Gaine, C and George, R (1999) *Gender, 'Race' and Class in Schooling: A New Introduction*. London: RoutledgeFalmer

Holland, V (1998) 'Underachieving Boys: Problems and Solutions' *Support for Learning* 13(4), pages 174–178

Kelly, A (1986) *Gender Differences in Teacher-Pupil Interaction: A Meta-analytical Review*. Paper presented at the British Educational Research Association Annual Conference, Bristol, September

Murray, J (2009) *20th Century Britain: The Woman's Hour* **www.bbc.co.uk/history/british/modern/jmurray_01.shtml**

Oakley, A (2005) *The Ann Oakley Reader: Gender, Women and Social Science*. Bristol: The Policy Press

Paechter, C (1998) *Educating the Other: Gender, Power and Schooling.* Abingdon: RoutledgeFalmer.

Skelton, C and Francis, B (2009) *Feminism and 'the schooling scandal'*. Abingdon: Routledge.

Younger, M and Warrington, M (2007) 'Closing the Gender Gap? Issues of Gender Equity in English Secondary Schools', *Discourse: Studies in the Cultural Politics of Education*, (28:22), pages 19–242

Weiner, G (1994) *Feminism in Education*. Buckingham: Open University Press

Arnot, M, David, M and Weiner, G (1999) *Closing the Gender Gap: Postwar Education and Social Change.* Cambridge: Polity Press

Connolly, P (2004) *Boys and Schooling in the Early Years.* Abingdon: Routledge.

Skelton, C, Francis, B and Smulyan, L (eds) (2006) *The SAGE handbook of gender and education.* London: Sage

http://nationalstrategies.standards.dcsf.gov.uk/genderandachievement/
www.genderandeducation.com/

www.education.gov.uk – New Department for Education

Chapter 7
Ethnicity, race and culture

OBJECTIVES

By the end of this chapter you should have:
- understood some of the difficulties involved in using terms such as race, racism, culture and ethnicity;
- examined the charge that formal systems of education in Britain are *institutionally racist*;
- recognised differences between theories of *underachievement* and *educational disadvantage* and considered the usefulness of each;
- identified intersections between identities and inequalities built around race or ethnicity and those built around gender and socio-economic class.

Introduction

Terms such as race, racism, ethnicity, culture or cultural community are often used by commentators reporting on the educational experience and achievement of different student groups. This chapter begins by reflecting on where these terms have come from, what they mean, and what help they might offer us in understanding patterns of inequality in Britain's schools. Extract one considers the claim that Britain's formal system of education is *institutionally racist* while Extracts two and three illustrate rather different responses to this charge.

Concerning language

In books such as this, it has become almost obligatory for the word *race* to appear in quotation marks – or 'scare-marks' – to warn readers, 'we don't think this word means what you might think it does'. Some of the most common or everyday understandings of the term imply that a 'race' is a biological classification for people who share certain physical characteristics. However, the genetic significance of 'race' as a category has been resoundingly rejected by the scientific community: there are many more differences *within* supposed *racial groups* than there are between. In fact, many scholars now argue that the idea that humanity is split into separate 'races' is a creation of the racist imagination which fuelled the development of Western European colonialism and transatlantic slavery (Gilroy, 2000). The quotation marks therefore signify that 'race' is about imagined or *socially constructed* difference rather than something biological or innate (after Lewis and Phoenix, 2004). Some people have argued that the term should no longer be used at all. However, *although 'race' is a social construct, it has real effects: it continues to be treated as socially significant because inequalities are reproduced through practices of racism* (Lewis and Phoenix, 2004, page 125).

'Race' might not exist in reality but *racism* – the unequal treatment of some people on the basis of *perceived* racial difference – certainly does.

Gaine and George (1999, page 5) suggest that *ethnicity* is a *far more preferable* term than 'race' *because it unambiguously refers to culture* rather than making any claims on the basis of nature or biology: *An ethnic group is simply a group which shares certain cultural features such as language, religion, various customs, perhaps food and clothing prefer- ences. It usually depends on a sense of shared peoplehood – that is to say that if a group believe themselves to be an ethnic group based on one or more of the above features then they probably are.*

However, the term 'ethnicity' is not without its own problems. A number of commenta- tors have suggested that over the last three decades, a new form of cultural racism has emerged in which *crude biological doctrines and stereotypes of innate superiority/inferi- ority* have given way *to a more subtle and indirect discourse* that speaks about *cultural differences as an 'organic' principle of discrimination.* (Cohen, 1999, page 4). Within this newer discourse, 'ethnicity' can be used as though it refers to clear and discrete ethnic groups whose members will automatically share the same norms and values and who will inevitably see and do things differently from members of other groups. Lewis and Phoenix suggest that the terms *racialisation* and *ethnicisation* – or *racialised* and *ethnicised* identi- ties – could be used instead:

> *Firstly, [these terms] place an emphasis on the social and psychological processes involved in putting individuals and groups into 'racial' or 'ethnic' categories. Secondly this means that the terms 'race' and 'ethnicity' are no longer seen to be natural or fixed, but as identities that result from particular ways of seeing people.*

> (Lewis and Phoenix, 2004, page 123)

Critically, the boundaries between both 'ethnic groups' and 'racial groups' are neither fixed nor clear. *Where one draws the line . . .depends on who is drawing the line and for what purpose* (Gaine and George 1999, page 5). In extract one, for example, the authors have consciously decided to use just two terms: 'Black' and 'White'. They explain that *the word Black (with a capital letter) is used ... to refer to people targeted by racism*, and because it is, *the preferred way which many people adopt – people of South Asian origin as well as African or Caribbean origin – to define their own identity, and to summarise the experiences, struggles and objectives which they have in common* (Richardson and Wood 2000, page x).

Some publications use the term BME – Black and Minority Ethnic – in a similar manner. But in other contexts, much greater precision is required. For example, we may want to explore the differences in school experience, not just between people of African Caribbean and South Asian origin but *within* those groups: between Indian, Pakistani and Bangladeshi origin communities, or between first generation African Caribbean immi- grants and those of African Caribbean heritage who were born and raised in Britain.

'Ethnicity' and 'race' in British schools

Britain has long been a destination for migrating settlers from across the world and historical records suggest that there has been a continuous Black population resident here since at least the sixteenth century. However, the post-war period of invited immigration from former British colonies is seen to mark a significant turning point in the country's social and demographic history. By the end of the 1960s, many British cities were home to firmly established African Caribbean and South Asian communities. A second generation of Black Britons were being born and raised here and were being sent to British schools. By the 1970s, concerns that certain groups of students were underperforming relative to others had already begun to emerge. In 1971, Grenadian born Bernard Coard published a pamphlet entitled, *How the West Indian Child is Made Educationally Sub-Normal in the British School System* (reproduced in Richardson, 2005). In it he detailed the significant over-representation of Black children in referrals to Educational Sub-normal Schools for those considered to have special educational needs.

Early explanations for West Indian students' (as they were then labelled) *underperformance* tended to locate the blame and/or responsibility either with the students themselves or with their wider cultural communities. Spurious genetic explanations regarding the inherent intelligence of different groups were offered but then largely rejected only to be replaced by explanations which blamed alleged impoverishments in African Caribbean culture and family life or else argued that individual Black students had a supposedly deficient sense of self-esteem (for a useful summary see Nehaul, 1996). The emerging recognition that Asian (in fact, primarily Indian) students appeared to be performing particularly well within the school system only served to reinforce these arguments. For example, the high profile 1985 Swann Report suggested that *the reasons for the very different school performances of Asians and West Indians seem likely to lie within their respective cultures* (page 87). While Asian pupils were characterised in terms of keeping their heads down, adopting a low profile and belonging to communities which were tight-knit, respectful and supportive, West Indians were characterised in contrast as being likely to protest and assume a high profile and as belonging to communities which were disrespectful, dysfunctional and irreverent (DES, 1985, page 86, and CCCS, 1982).

Coard's publication was one of the first public suggestions that at least *some* blame or responsibility might in fact lie within the education system. By 1985, even the Swann report acknowledged that British schools – and wider British society – might constitute a hostile environment for a minority ethnic child. Throughout the 1980s and 1990s this argument gained momentum as a growing number of empirical studies suggested that the notion of *underperformance,* or in today's language *underachievement,* was not the right way to frame the issue and attention should instead be paid to the ways that some students were being disadvantaged by their schools. Such studies attempted to illustrate the existence of low teacher expectations, stereotyped teaching materials, culturally biased curricula and/or disproportionate criticism and control directed at certain student groups, (for a fuller discussion see Nehaul, 1996 and Gaine and George, 1999). However, this perspective remained contentious (Foster 1990) and although the same decades witnessed increased antiracist and multicultural interventions in many local authorities and schools, the claim that the whole education system served to disadvantage Black and minority ethnic students did not receive overwhelming popular or political support.

Then, in February 1999, the Macpherson report was published, detailing the failures and inadequacies of the British police and criminal justice system in response to the fatal stabbing of Black British teenager Stephen Lawrence in 1993. Extract 1 is taken from a book written in response to the Stephen Lawrence Inquiry and considers the implications of the report for Britain's schools.

EXTRACT ONE

Richardson, R and Wood, A (2000) Inclusive Schools, Inclusive Society. *Stoke on Trent: Trentham, pages 28, 33, 35*

The report by Sir William Macpherson concluded that the unprofessional conduct of police officers was due not merely to inefficiency or to a chapter of accidents, but to what it called institutional racism. 'There must be an unequivocal acceptance,' said the report, 'of the problem of institutional racism and its nature, before it can be addressed, as it needs to be, in full partnership with members of minority ethnic communities.'

When he introduced the report in the House of Commons on 24 February 1999, the Home Secretary observed that institutional racism is a feature of all government departments, and all areas of society: 'Any long-established, White-dominated organisation is liable to have procedures, practices and a culture which tends to exclude or disadvantage non-white people. The police service in this respect is little different from other parts of the criminal justice system, or from government departments ... and many other institutions.' The education system – amongst many other systems – stood accused.

[...]

Key terms and phrases [from the Inquiry's attempt to defined 'institutional racism'] can be used to compile a statement about racism in education as follows:

In the education system there are laws, customs and practices which systematically reflect and reproduce racial inequalities ... If racist consequences accrue to institutional laws, customs and practices, a school or a local education authority or a national education system is racist whether or not individual teachers, inspectors, officers, civil servants and elected politicians have racist intentions ... Educational institutions may systematically treat or tend to treat pupils and students differently in respect of race, ethnicity or religion. The differential treatment lies within an institution's ethos and organisation rather than in the attitudes, beliefs and intentions of individual members of staff. The production of differential treatment is 'institutionalised' in the way the institution operates'.

Racial inequality in institutions – dimensions and examples

Dimensions of inequality	Examples of inequality in the criminal justice system	Examples of inequality in the education system
OUTCOMES White people receive more benefits than Black, and racial inequality is therefore perpetuated.	Crimes against White people are investigated and cleared up more effectively than crimes against Black people.	White pupils leave school at 16 or 18 with substantially better qualifications than Black people.
Black people receive negative results more than do White people and in this way too inequality is perpetuated.	Black people are far more likely than White people to be stopped and searched by the police.	Black pupils experience punishments, particularly permanent and fixed term exclusions more than White pupils.
STRUCTURE In senior decision-making and policy making positions there are proportionately more White people than Black, and in consequence Black interests and perspectives are inadequately represented.	There are few Black officers at or above the rank of Inspector, and also few Black people in the rest of the criminal justice system.	There are few Black headteachers or deputy heads, and few Black education officers, inspectors, teacher trainers and textbook writers.
CULTURE AND ATTITUDES In the occupational culture there are assumptions, expectations and generalisations which are more negative about Black people than about White.	Black people are more likely than White people to be seen as criminals or potential criminals.	Black pupils are more likely than White pupils to be seen as trouble-makers, and to be criticised and controlled.
RULES AND PROCEDURES Customary rules, regulations and practices work more to the advantage of White people than Black.	Throughout the criminal justice system Black people are treated less favourably than White people.	The national curriculum reflects White interests, concern and outlooks and neglects or marginalises Black experience.
STAFF TRAINING Staff have not received training on race and racism issues, and on ways they can avoid indirect discrimination.	Police officers have not been trained to identify and investigate racist attacks.	Neither initial no[r] inservice training pays sufficient attention to race and racism issues.
FACE-TO-FACE INTERACTION Staff are less effective in communication with and listening to Black people than they are in interaction with White people.	Encounters between White police officers and Black members of the public frequently escalate into needless confrontation.	Encounters between White staff and Black pupils frequently escalate into needless confrontation.

- *How convincing do you believe is the charge of institutional racism within the education system? What other information or forms of evidence might you require in order to decide?*

- *Consider each of the dimensions of inequality outlined in Box 24. Which do you think most important to address? How might the education system be able to do so?*

Ethnic monitoring and examination success

It is currently a statutory requirement for local authorities to collect and submit data on the ethnicity of school students in line with current (2001) census categories. This has enabled policy-makers and analysts to record patterns of inequality in student attainment at different Key Stage benchmarks, to identify incidence of pupil improvement or decline between Key Stages, to highlight regional (local or even school-based) variation and to demonstrate changes over time. In this short chapter it is impossible to do justice to the complexity that different forms of analysis are able to reveal (see for example Gillborn and Mirza, 2000; Connolly, 2006; Strand, 2007). However, just a few snap-shot figures from the 2008/9 GCSE results for England suggest that, ten years after Richardson and Wood were writing, there still appears to be considerable cause for concern. While, across all pupils, 50.7 per cent achieved 5 or more A*–C grade passes, this was true of only 39.4 per cent of Black Caribbean pupils, 42.3 per cent of mixed race White and Black Caribbean pupils and 42.9 per cent of pupils of Pakistani heritage (DCSF, 2010).

In the 2008 book from which extract two is taken, David Gillborn argues that in Britain, not only does education policy continue to fail to address these inequalities, it actually sustains them. In the extract below he examines a return within popular discourse to explanations which draw on cultural comparisons between different minority ethnic groups.

EXTRACT TWO

Gillborn, D (2008) Racism and Education: Coincidence or Conspiracy? *Abingdon: Routledge, pages 152–155*

Model minorities: the benefit to the status quo

I have already indicated some of the ways in which the achievement of Indian and Chinese students is positioned in public debates on race and education: at this point it is worth considering the process a little further. The public image of successful hard-working Indian and Chinese students has become a discursive resource that is deployed whenever the question of racism in education is raised. There are two key ways in which this happens: first, the mere fact of minority success is positioned as if it automatically disproves the charge of racism against any and all minoritized groups; and second, comparisons are made with 'underachieving' groups so that the latter are cast as deficient and even dangerous.

The notion of institutional racism, as operationalized in the Lawrence Inquiry report, has been subject to huge controversy and wilful misrepresentation [. .]. Although the concept clearly attempts to recognize the complex (sometimes hidden) nature of racism, a great deal of White comment seems to ignore this dimension and equate every mention of 'racism' with race hatred of the most conscious, violent and one-dimensional kind. Within this simplistic world view any minority success is assumed to be incompatible with the charge of racism:

> *Whatever failings teachers have, racism – institutional or otherwise – is not one of them ... We have known for some time that in secondary schools, pupils of Asian and Chinese origin make better progress than their white peers. (Professor Anthony O'Hear, 1999)*

The infamous definition, produced by the Macpherson inquiry into the murder of Stephen Lawrence, is demonstrably ridiculous here. For the report shows that while Bangladeshi and black Caribbean children do worse than white children, Indians and Chinese do very much better. It's a strange kind of institutional racism that actually favours some ethnic minorities. (Melanie Phillips, 1999)

I'm no educationist, but if you examine the statistics it is certainly difficult to conclude that our schools discriminate against ethnic minorities, even unwittingly. Chinese and some other Asian pupils excel, easily outperforming the whites. (Rod Liddle, 2005)

Reading statements like these it is sometimes difficult to believe that the opinions are serious: do commentators (regardless of their own Whiteness and lack of research understanding) genuinely think that success by one or two minority groups necessarily disproves the presence of racism across the board? Are they really so convinced of the system's colour-blind meritocratic principles? Each of the writers noted above has been an outspoken critic of the state education system and yet they cannot conceive that some minoritized groups are systematically discriminated against in the same system they are so swift to decry at other times (on other topics). These quotations are especially revealing because each of the articles references the Lawrence Inquiry, either directly or indirectly, and yet completely fails to understand even the most basic reality of how racism operates. Statements such as these trade on the crudest possible notion of racism and are entirely at odds with the research evidence from schools.

As I have noted, there is a large and growing body of work that clearly documents how teachers' perspectives differ depending on the particular minoritized group they are deal-ing with. Racists have always played favourites, viewing some groups as exotic, mysterious and alluring, while others are seen as bestial, savage and threatening: the same processes are at play in contemporary classrooms and staffrooms (Brah, 1992; Delgado and Stefancic, 2001). The exceptionally high expectations that many teachers hold about Indian and Chinese students are the flip side of the same coin that involves the demonization of Black students. Indeed, many commentators and 'experts' display these same tendencies in their readiness to use the model minority stereotype of Indian and Chinese students as licence to further denigrate and assault Black students, their parents and communities:

There's certainly not institutional racism ... If Indian children are doing better than white children then there is not institutional racism. We have to look at the particu-lar groups themselves and wonder what's happening there. (Professor James Tooley in Blair et al, 1999: 10, emphasis added.)

Asian and Chinese pupils still manage to get more out of the school experience than do black boys. Alan Hall, a Bradford head teacher, believes: 'The biggest single advantage [Asian pupils] gain from their family background is that they are seldom cynical about school, teachers and education.'(Yasmin Alibhai-Brown, 2000: 4, emphasis added.)

What these perspectives fail to understand is the absolutely vital importance of education for very many of the minoritized groups that appear at the wrong end of the league table hierarchy. The Black British community, for example, has an exemplary history of mobiliza-tion around educational issues, not only pushing for better standards in the state system but also organizing and funding literally thousands of 'supplementary' and 'Saturday' schools run by the community, for the community (John, 2006; Mirza and Reay, 2000; Reay and Mirza 1997; Richardson, 2005). But this commitment – whilst at least as deep as any other groups' – does not always surface in ways that match the expectations of White teachers and other observers. The headteacher quoted by Yasmin Alibhai-Brown is especially interesting because of his reference to 'cynicism'. Research with Black students and parents, in the US and the UK, reveals a degree of understanding and wariness that might be viewed (incorrectly) as cynicism by some, but is perhaps more accurately viewed as a realistic understanding of past injustices and current mistreatments. Jan McKenley's life history research with Black 40-something fathers, for example, reveals the vital but complex place that education holds within their lives as parents and as ex-students:

> *When I sat my maths exam at school, one look at the paper told me that I was not equipped to do it, to pass it so I left after a few minutes. I knew I was going to fail, so I take control. (Owen)*

> *My kids know that I am in private aggressively pro-black and condemning of white racism and so debates around subjects become quite lively at home ... My kids watched me as I did my MBA [Master of Business Administration] and my son, in particular who is good at maths, was roped in to help me with the mathematics in the MBA. They have a sense that there are benefits to be gained. So he knows it's to be strived for. I said to him don't be doing yours at my age, do bits of study but get the bulk of it out of your way while you're young. (Dennis)*

> *I make my guidance explicit and I insist on homework being done. I make my expectations and goals explicit and encourage my children to do the same. (Devon)*

> *(McKenley, 2005: 112–14)*

Similarly, Lorna Cork's work with Black parents and students powerfully demonstrates that many parents, especially fathers, are deeply involved in their children's education but sometimes in ways that are not immediately visible to schools, who assume that absence at a parents' evening denotes an absent or uninterested parent and are unaware of the myriad complex constraints that can prevent such overt displays (Cork, 2005). None of this should come as a surprise: migrant communities frequently look to education as a way of cementing their future. The commitments of 'model minorities' are no more impressive than those of less successful and more maligned groups: Exhibit 7.3, for example, provides the most powerful evidence possible, in this case relating to an 'asylum seeker'; a group defined in current British popular and political discourses as among the least deserving and most Othered of groups.

Exhibit 7. 3

> *'I want my son Antonio to stay in the UK to continue his studies'*

> *So read a note found after Manuel Bravo, a 35-year-old asylum seeker, hung himself at the Yarl's Wood Detention Centre, Bedfordshire, the day before he expected to be forcibly repatriated to Angola.*

Mr Bravo's son Antonio, aged 13 at the time of his father's death, will now be able to stay in England until he is 18, when he will be able to apply for asylum.

Mr Bravo's parents, who had links to a political opposition group, were murdered in Angola in 2001. Mr Bravo's wife and youngest child had returned briefly to Angola, so that she could care for a recently orphaned niece: they were imprisoned for two months and then fled to a neighbouring country.

At his first tribunal hearing in England Mr Bravo represented himself because his solicitor failed to show. Contemporary newspaper reports suggest that Mr Bravo and his son were taken into custody at 6am when police broke into their house. At that point there had still been no official result from his earlier asylum hearing, making his removal to the detention centre illegal.

A year later the inquest heard that a note left for Antonio read: 'Be a good son and do well at school.'

Sources: BBC News Online (2006); Herbert (2005); Pallister (2006)

POINTS TO CONSIDER

- *David Gillborn resoundingly rejects the argument, but what do you think about the suggestion that the relative success of certain groups of Asian students disproves the existence of institutional racism in British schools?*

- *What other explanations might be missing for these students' apparent success?*

- *Can you think of any costs to individual students from model minority groups?*

Complicating the picture: intersections of race, ethnicity, gender and class

As Gillborn points out, it is important to recognise that the social structure of Britain is such that identities and inequalities built around race or ethnicity very often intersect with inequalities of social class. Ethnicity (and/or cultural background) is not the only contributing factor to Indian and Chinese students' relative academic success: *official indicators of social disadvantage are lowest for these two groups*, there are proportionately fewer Indian or Chinese students on free school meals and Indians students are the group most likely to be privately educated (Gillborn, 2008, page 147).

Gillborn does note that even when Chinese or Indian students *do* meet indicators of poverty, they still tend to achieve more highly than their peers, but his argument is that this by no means disproves the existence of racism. Even ostensibly positive stereotypes can trap students in an essentialist and racialising discourse. Gillborn cites a number of classroom-based research projects which illustrate how hard it can be for both Indian and Chinese students to claim and create a self-identity outside of teachers', and other students' ethnic stereotypes (see for example Youdel, 2006; Archer and Francis ,2005a). Supposed success stories for *model minorities* which are narrowly defined in terms of examination performance can also ignore the racially motivated verbal and/or physical abuse which research evidence suggests many of these students continue to experience (Archer and Francis, 2005b).

These and other recent ethnographic studies also emphasise a further intersection between racialising or ethnicising discourses and gendered identities in schools. Archer and Francis, for example, describe how the majority of the teachers that they interviewed positioned their ideas of typical Chinese British boys' behaviour as different to *normal* or *laddish masculinity* (2005b). Similarly, research conducted within students' peer-group cultures has documented that Asian boys are regularly constructed as *not properly masculine, passive* and, as a possible consequence, *unpopular* by their contemporaries (Phoenix, 2004, page 240). The same research also suggests that Black boys are commonly expected and encouraged to perform a form of *super* or *hyper masculinity* demonstrating physical prowess, being *strong, tough* and *hard*, being *cool* and independent and acting in a manner antithetical to getting on in school (Frosh, Phoenix and Pattman, 2002). Although these forms of behaviour may ultimately damage their academic achievement, they simultaneously appear to offer alternative sources of status and esteem.

The same observation has been made by Tony Sewell, one of the two contributors whose voices you will hear in extract three. In recent years, Sewell has contested the claim that Black boys' academic achievement is only determined by school-based institutional racism and his arguments have courted considerable controversy.

EXTRACT THREE

Jasper, J and Sewell, T (2003) 'Look Beyond the Street' (email exchange hosted by the Guardian newspaper website, at www.guardian.co.uk/world/2003/jul/19/race.raceineducation)

Dear Lee, *According to this week's Voice newspaper, the Commission for Racial Equality [now replaced by the Equality and Human Rights Commission] is going after those schools that have failed to comply with the 2000 Race Relations Act and produce a robust equality policy. I welcome this action, but doubt whether it will get to the core reasons why black children underachieve in our schools.*

Many black head teachers and black students are clear that underachievement can be due to the individual student, parents, community, peers and, of course, school. They don't agree that poverty and institutionalised racism are the most important factors. I would go further and say that political correctness has avoided the real issue of an anti-school black masculinity that pervades not only our inner city but those black boys who attend schools in the suburbs.

When it comes to the CRE challenging failing schools, its remit must be wider than just white racism. It must also challenge a youth culture that still thinks to do well in school is to "act white". **Tony**

I welcome the CRE's stated intention. Far too many schools have refused to seriously tackle institutional racism within the classroom and the playground. As a parent and, for the last six years, a school governor, I am acutely aware of the disproportionate levels of underachievement of black boys; differential exclusion rates, failure to develop a culturally appropriate curriculum, and the failure to recruit black teachers and governors.

Criminal levels of unemployment have immersed our community in poverty, confining us to some of the most deprived wards in the UK. While it is important to identify peer pressure and cultural influences as a factor, one should not make the mistake of identifying the symptoms as the cause.

The historical and continued stereotypical demonisation of black men is the problem leading to the behaviour that you ascribe to a cultural trait of "anti-school black masculinity". I have just finished teaching bicycle road safety to my seven-year-old son where I emphasised the importance of wearing his helmet. Yesterday, as I was having my dinner, I heard him talking to someone at the front door. It was a white motorcyclist who thought my son had threatened to cut his throat. As this man had approached our house, my son had noticed that his helmet had not been secured under his chin and had pointed this out by drawing his finger across his throat. The motorcyclist had interpreted this piece of public safety advice as a threat, and had stopped to remonstrate with my son.

This is what racism does to black boys. It assumes the worst and over-reacts. **Lee Jasper**

Dear Lee *Of course the CRE must do its duty, but let's stay focused. When we were at school, there was a definite system of apartheid that meant that many of us were dumped in Special Needs Units or told we could only do CSEs. I was talking to a head teacher recently who said that when it came to access, black boys today have real opportunities that they are failing to grasp. I talk to middle class, black parents who tell me they literally have to fight to keep their boys on task. These are boys from well-resourced homes, they go to the better state schools and yet they are performing below their potential.*

I feel that you don't want to address this issue because it isn't politically expedient for you. The anecdote about your son is nothing compared to what I experienced as a child on my way back and forth from my primary school when I would have to run the gauntlet of racial abuse.

This generation has it easy compared to our day. A black male today faces anti-school peer pressure that dominates our schools. Ask your son about it if you need some enlightenment. Today a head teacher told me how one student was jumped outside of his school: he was beaten and his attackers took his mobile phone, his trainers, his jacket and his cap. In our inner cities, black male youth culture has moved from a community of safety and brotherhood to one of fear of each other. This culture has little time for school or homework.

I have no doubt that teacher racism is alive in our schools, but it can't explain the depth and breadth of this underachievement. Come on, Lee! You've proved your anti-racist credentials. There's a whole set of young black men who are looking for a motivational leadership that speaks to their particular needs.

EXTRACT THREE continued

Come and join me. The gospel I preach is a simple one. It asks black young men to look beyond the street and beyond immediate gratification. It asks some hard questions about their own responsibilities: homework, bedtime, respect for peers and adults, good manners, self-control and how to succeed in the system. Nobody is asking our boys these questions. We just get more politicians telling them they're victims of racism. **Tony**

Like most working-class communities, those who have endured long-term poverty develop a counter-culture that seeks to offer validation where society and schools fail to do so. You are obsessed by a black middle class that does not exist in any real sense.

I am not seeking to compare my son's experience with your own, or anyone else's. The example highlights the world as black boys experience it, and it is largely a world that is defined by white people's thoughts, attitudes and expectations – or lack of them. You are seeking to underplay historically powerful social forces like racism and poverty, and reduce them to a substantive definitive character or cultural defect of black communities.

At school I was both badly beaten and, sadly, inflicted bad beatings on others. It was part and parcel of the experience of living in a poor community. I am not sure why you treat this as some sort of unique contemporary phenomena within black culture. If our young men glorify 'street culture' then it's because they have been brought up to be perfect consumers of that culture. Mercedes, Gucci, Platinum Ice and a penthouse – this is the dream they have been sold. These are children from families that have been crushed under the colossal weight of long-term deprivation – single parents, teenage pregnancies and a community that cannot get gainful employment.

I will resist your invitation to join your postmodernist church. Yours is a false and diverse doctrine. I see black young people who exhibit all the characteristics of mature self-responsibility every single day. As a member of the Mayor of London's African Caribbean Education Commission looking at the educational performance of black boys, I have become routinely depressed at the articulation of our young people in relation to their current experience of secondary education. Over and over again we heard the same story: of discipline regulations differentially applied, never being picked to answer a question; teachers with no understanding of their pupils' cultural background, favouritism of white children above black children; blatant and covert racism. This is further reinforced by black teachers and head teachers whose experience is largely one of marginalisation and lost opportunity.

Of course I accept that there are kids who are problematic, but self-responsibility will not in itself defeat institutional racism in schools.

The failure to answer difficult questions relates rather more to those who are in government than it does to young black people. **Lee Jasper**

***My dear Lee**, You seem to sidestep what I am saying. It is patronising to tell a people whose ancestors fought against the deep horror of the slave system that they can't be motivated to see the value of using education.*

We as African and Caribbean people have always known poverty, but we have always had the spirit to challenge it. Much of our poverty is real, but I'm talking about a huge cohort of black boys who are not on the breadline but whose homes are impoverished. In these homes you will see huge television sets, cable TV, wardrobes with the latest designer wear, yet not one book. Don't lecture me about poverty, Lee. I came from the same plantation as many of these children. We had to rush out each night to buy paraffin to light the only fire in our rented room. I'm sorry, they don't know racism and poverty like my generation knew it.

The real poverty that our children face is a poverty of aspiration – they have linked themselves with the prevailing anti-learning culture of their white working class counterparts. The sin that you commit is to give this "mentality" credence by reducing it solely to white racism. This for me is the new slave mentality, the one that keeps us from seeing that, irrespective of the pressure, you do have the ability to succeed. What are we supposed to do in the meantime, Lee? Wait for white people to change so that we can be free? I am convinced that teachers' fear and racism is holding our children back, but not defeating them.

I have just completed a fascinating piece of research in Hackney schools. I gave a questionnaire to 11-year-old black Caribbean boys, who had just completed their SATS tests. I asked them about the kind of support they had at home – bedtimes, books in the home, etc. Almost to a boy, those who got level 4-plus had home support. Those who got level 3 had no help.

*We need to resource black parents to help their own children and you, Lee, need to read a book called Up from Slavery by Booker T Washington. It's what we buppie black folks read before bedtime!! **Tony Sewell***

***Tony**, Levels of racial inequality have grown in education, health, criminal justice and public sector employment over the last 20 years. This indicates that racism has increased over this time. The greatest weapon in the hands of an oppressor is the mind of the oppressed, and your blind refusal to correctly assess the impact of racism lets all white people off the hook.*

*That working class, black parents can get their priorities wrong in terms of material possession is a distinctly human trait not confined to our community. Yes, there are some homes without books, but there are many more with them. **Lee Jasper***

POINTS TO CONSIDER

- *On what points do Lee Jasper and Tony Sewell seem to reach an agreement and on what points do they most strongly disagree?*

- *Whose position do you find most convincing?*

- *Can you identify any similarities and differences between Tony Sewell's arguments here and those earlier explanations which located blame for Black students' educational performance within Black communities themselves?*

Sewell, Jasper and other contributors to ongoing debate and discussion concerning Black boys' education raise some difficult but important questions. Unlike earlier explanations which served to pathologise Black students and their families, Sewell argues that he is resisting the trend within recent educational discourse to position ethnic minority students as simply the victims of racism in schools or society. He wants to return some sense of agency and the power that can come with responsibility to Black communities.

C H A P T E R   S U M M A R Y

This chapter has warned against the unreflexive use of terms such as 'race' and 'ethnicity' and suggested that concepts such as *racialisation* and *ethnicisation* might be more appropriate. These latter terms recognise a centrally important argument of the chapter: racial or ethnic identities are actively constructed within schools by teachers and by students and in relation to wider social inequalities. The chapter highlighted that there are intersections between racialising or ethnicising discourses and both gendered and class-based identities. Statistical evidence which highlights the scale of underperformance and/or disadvantage among certain students is important but can serve to obscure such complexity.

REFERENCES

Archer, L and Francis, B (2005a) 'Constructions of Racism by British Chinese Pupils and Parents'. Race, *Ethnicity and Education*, 8(4), pp387–407

Archer, L and Francis, B (2005b) 'They never go off the rails like other ethnic minority groups': Teachers' constructions of British Chinese pupils' gender identities and approaches to learning', *British Journal of the Sociology of Education*, 26(2) pp165–182

Centre for Contemporary Cultural Studies (CCCS) (1982) *The empire strikes back*. London: Hutchinson

Cohen, P (ed.) (1999) *New ethnicities: old racisms*. London: Zed Books

Connolly, P (2006) Summary statistics, educational achievement gaps and the ecological fallacy. *Oxford Review of Education*, 32 (2), pp235–52

DCSF (2010) *Key Stage 4 attainment by pupil characteristics: Statistical first release.* [online] 4 March 2010. www.dcsf.gov.uk/rsgateway/DB/SFR/s000900/SFR34_2009Revised.pdf

Department for Education and Sciences (DES) (1985) *Education for all* (The Swann Report). London: HMSO

Foster, P (1990) 'Cases not proven: an evaluation of two studies of teacher racism' *British Educational Research Journal*, 16(4), pp335–349

Frosh, S, Phoenix, A and Pattman, R (2002) *Young Masculinities*. Basingstoke: Palgrave

Gaine, C and George, R (1999) *Gender, 'race' and class in schooling: a new introduction*. London: RoutledgeFalmer

Gillborn, D. and Mirza, H.S. (2000) *Educational inequality: mapping race, class and gender*. London: OFSTED

Gilroy, P (2000) *Between camps: nations, cultures and the allure of race*. London: Penguin

Lewis, G and Phoenix, A (2004) '"Race", "ethnicity" and "identity"' in K Woodward (ed) *Questioning identity: gender, class, ethnicity*. London: Routledge

Nehaul, K (1996) *The schooling of children of Caribbean heritage*. Stoke-on-Trent: Trentham

Phoenix, A (2004) 'Neoliberalism and masculinity: racialization and the contradictions of schooling for 11–14 year olds'. *Youth & Society* 36(2), pp227–249

Strand, S (2007) *Minority ethnic pupils in the longitudinal study of young people in England* (LSYPE. Nottingham: Department for Schools, Children & Families

Youdell (2006) *Impossible bodies, impossible selves: exclusions and student subjectivities*. Dordrecht, Netherlands: Springer

FURTHER READING

Ladson-Billings, G and Gillborn, D (eds) (2004) *The RoutledgeFalmer Reader in Multicultural Education*. London: RoutledgeFalmer

Richardson, B (ed) (2005) *Tell it like it is: How our schools fail black children*. Stoke-on-Trent: Trentham

Sewell, T (2009) *Generating genius: Black boys in search of love, ritual and schooling*. Stoke-on-Trent: Trentham

WEBSITES

www.standards.dfes.gov.uk/ethnicminorities/ – Ethnic Minority Achievement pages on the DCSF Standards Site

www.runnymedetrust.org – The Runnymede Trust is an independent voluntary organisation which commissions and collates research on many aspects of life in multi-ethnic Britain including education.

www.insted.co.uk/ – Insted aims to support educational development and training related to equality and diversity issues in British schools.

www.education.gov.uk – New Department for Education

Chapter 8

Special educational needs and inclusive education

OBJECTIVES

By the end of this chapter you should have:
- identified different models of disability and considered the ways in which disability is socially constructed;
- reflected upon the arguments for and against *mainstreaming* and specialist provision for children with special educational needs;
- critically analysed the notion of inclusion, with particular reference to inclusive assessment practices.

Introduction

The term special educational needs derived from the Warnock Report (1978) and this informed the 1981 Education Act. Since that time, there has been an increasing emphasis on the quality and scope of educational provision – the extent to which mainstream schools, colleges and universities can be and are equipped with appropriate resources, specialist equipment and training to cater for the needs of children with special educational needs. Over time, forms of provision have transformed and the focus of attention has broadened.

Before the 1980s, children with physical disabilities were provided with education in segregated, specialist institutions. The 1981 act implemented, where it was deemed fitting, the integration of children who had previously been segregated into mainstream institutions. The concept of 'learning difficulties' was advanced to take into account a wide continuum of educational needs – developing categories of learning difficulties such as emotional and behavioural, moderate, severe and complex, profound and multiple. Educators increasingly understood and defined children's educational experiences in terms of specific learning difficulties – dyslexia, dyspraxia, autism, Asperger syndrome and attention deficit and hyperactivity disorder – each incorporating a complex and wide-ranging spectrum of patterns of behaviour and learning needs. In 2008, around 20 per cent of pupils in compulsory-age schooling were categorised as having special educational needs (SEN) – 2.7 per cent with statements (a document outlining the assessment of need and the required provision) and 17.8 per cent without (DCSF, 2009). Currently, the inclusion agenda promotes effective learning opportunities for all so that schools are responsive to the diverse needs of *all* children, whether disabled, with learning difficulties, from deprived background, ethnic minorities, with English as an additional language or 'gifted and talented'. This is a whole-school approach emphasising membership of and participation in the learning community.

To place this complex and fluid environment in context, the chapter begins by examining the social, cultural and economic barriers that have constructed disability and special educational needs. The chapter then focuses specifically on the debate that has come to dominate discussions within this field over recent years – the relative merits of segregated and mainstream provision for children with special educational needs. Finally, it focuses on the notion of inclusion and considers what this means in practice, the extent that current provision can be viewed as inclusive and the obstacles to a genuinely inclusive education system.

The construction of disability

The first extract examines how our understanding of disability has transformed over the centuries. The extract begins by identifying an important division, one you have come across in early chapters, between perceptions of 'normal' and 'other' – with the 'other' generally supposed to be beneath, or *sub*-'normal'. This division between 'normality' and 'otherness' is highly dependent on context – differing considerably according to time, place and setting and defined by prevailing values, attitudes and physical environments. This is indicative of the socially-constructed nature of disability: disability is shaped and constrained by social structures and cultures (how people commonly talk about and think about disability and the extent that society is organised to include or exclude) more than by physical impediments. Disability is constructed in the following ways:

- *definition* – the social, physical and mental conditions that are viewed as disabled;

- *language* – the labels and terms used to describe disabled people;

- *explanation* – the perceived causes of disability, whether spiritual, religious, medical, social or cultural;

- *response* – the judgements, entitlements, treatments or provision.

As you read the extract, you are likely to feel uneasy with some of the descriptions and language you come across. It is hard to envisage the traditions that constructed (defined, explained and treated) disability in our relatively recent history.

Mortimore, T (2008) 'Social and Educational Inclusion' in Ward, S. (ed.) (2008) A Student's Guide to Education Studies (2nd Edition). Abingdon: Routledge, pages 40– 43

Models of disability have influenced its depiction in the western world. A crucial element of this model was the distinction between what is 'normal' and what is 'other' – what is like me, and therefore 'family', what is not and therefore 'alien'. This 'normal'/'other' distinction also plays a part in shaping our responses to excluded groups, such as refugees, travellers or other ethnic minorities who subsequently become dehumanised and less worthy of sharing in our prosperity.

Barnes (1996) explored the cultural attitudes to disability throughout history. There is archaeological evidence of the existence of disability from the Neanderthal period and one utilitarian argument suggests that, in societies where survival is precarious, any individual unable to contribute would be seen as a liability and disposed of. However, Barnes provides examples of societies where people with impairments are both cared for and valued. He suggests that prejudice against people with impairments is not universal and that responses were culturally produced by complex relationships between the beliefs of the society and its social and economical structure.

The war-like, slave-based society of the Ancient Greeks glorified the physical toughness and perfection expressed in Greek statuary and the Olympic Games. Its obsession with bodily perfection introduced an ongoing bias against people with impairments in Western society. Those with disabilities received little help in Roman and Greek society. Charity developed haphazardly through the Christian church in Europe, which took the view that any individual not created in the perfect image of God was the product of the Devil and a punishment for the sins of mankind (Barnes, 1998). The notion was popularised through folk tales about changelings, dwarves, giants and ugly sisters and epitomised in the works of Shakespeare and other writers whose depiction of the impaired body created an impression of abnormality, damage and powerlessness or focused upon the hidden impairment of the 'diseased' mind. Think of the fate of Victor Hugo's Hunchback of Notre Dame, Shakespeare's black-hearted hunchbacked Richard III, the hook-handed Captain Hook in Peter Pan or the blinded and dependent Mr. Rochester in Jane Eyre.

Disability frequently signified moral ambivalence, evil, or childlike dependency. Dwarves and the 'feeble-minded' were the butt of jokes. Visits to Bedlam or the 'lunatic asylum' became entertainment and, by the Victorian era, the freak show was flourishing. Terms such as 'spastic' and 'moron' became insults. Darwin's theories of evolution, natural selection and the survival of the fittest produced Social Darwinism: the philosophy of sending the weak to the wall to benefit the majority. The Eugenics movement linked idiocy, poverty and criminality to heredity and argued that these 'degenerates' threatened society, should be kept separate to avoid contamination and sterilised to prevent their reproduction. These ideas were taken to the logical extreme by the Nazi party in Germany.

In the UK in 1870 the introduction of universal compulsory schooling increased pressure on schools through an influx of children from poorer families. Copeland (2003) points out that the Egerton Royal Commission (1886; 1889) suggested 5 per cent of urban children were *incapable of coping with elementary education and the school population was thus divided into two unequal groups. 'Exceptional children' or 'the dull and deficient' (Copeland, 2003: 45) were defined as 'imbeciles', condemned to pass their limited capabilities onto their descendants. They were identified by medical examination and placed in special schools with strictly limited curricula. Many did have impairments, but contemporary surveys suggested that disadvantages such as poverty, being orphaned, and being infected with heart and lung diseases affected many more. Their learning 'disabilities' sprang from the social, economic and environmental exclusion and from the brutal teaching and classroom discipline, rather than from their own impairment.*

The treatment of these children epitomises the 'medical model' of disability rooted in the individual's biology. It regards personal impairment and the individual's failure to adapt to society as the cause of disability. People are diagnosed by experts, usually medical or quasi-medical, who see all difficulties from the perspective of proposed treatments for patients. Disabled people are allocated the permanent sick role (Oliver, 1990), denied a voice, and relieved of responsibility and expectations. They are rendered dependent on 'experts' and forced to play the 'victim'. Experts make decisions about where they are educated, where they live, their employment, support or benefits available, and whether they can have children. The individual is pressured to cooperate, to abandon an impaired state that is regarded as 'less than human', to be rehabilitated into 'normal' functions or to be dismissed as 'incurable', dehumanised, identified by the disability, regarded as 'other' and punished by being excluded from ordinary life. This model is oppressive, frequently involving dominance and absence of choice. Up to ten years ago, people with disabilities were routinely excluded from the preparation of their own community care plans. The model also imposes both practical disadvantages and a 'discourse of disadvantage' onto people with disabilities. It is sometimes termed the 'disadvantage' model.

The medical model is constructed from a non-disabled or 'normal' standpoint and results in a society that segregates and establishes 'special' facilities away from community life, encouraging patronising attitudes, pity and fear. It has fuelled the market for the 'disability industry' (Barnes, 1996), particularly evident within education. It has encouraged the media representation of people with disabilities as 'other', dependent and of low social account. Some charities highlight this representation to incite a mixture of pity and guilt to potential donors, creating a dependent relationship between the (usually) non-disabled charity helpers and the disabled 'helped' and reducing the need for the state to be the prime mover in enabling people with disabilities to reach their potential.

The medical model became the dominant approach to the provision of services throughout much of the twentieth century. Although still dominant within NHS thinking, education and social service professions, it has been robustly challenged. The 1960s and 1970s saw struggles for civil liberties, in which people with disabilities increasingly participated. Social and economic structures began to be seen as contributing to the oppression of people with impairments. In the UK, the Union of Physically Impaired People Against Segregation (UPIAS, 1976) insisted that disabled people should speak for themselves and rejected the idea of 'experts' pronouncing on their behalf. UPIAS highlighted ways in which disabled people are discriminated against both by their exclusion from the material benefits of education and the economy and by the prejudice arising from cultural representations of disabled people as 'other'.

The emergence of post-modern theories and the work of philosophers such as Foucault (1980) sharpened awareness of the destructive nature of the current 'representations' of disability. Barton (1996) states that 'Disabled people's history needs to be viewed as part of an increasing struggle to establish and maintain positive self-identities' (p. 58). He distinguishes between impairment, physical or mental, possessed by an individual and the nature of disability and quotes the statement of Fundamental Principles of Disability taken from UPIAS and the Disabled Alliance.

> *In our view, it is society which disables physically impaired people. Disability is something imposed on top of our impairment by the way we are unnecessarily isolated and excluded from full participation in society. Disabled people are therefore an oppressed group in society.*

> *Thus we define impairment as lacking part or all of a limb, organ or mechanism of the body; and disability as the disadvantage or restriction of activity caused by a contemporary social organisation which takes no or little account of people who have physical impairments and thus excludes them from participation in the mainstream social activities. Physical impairment is therefore a particular form of oppression (p. 14, in Barton, 1996, p. 56).*

This is the 'social model', which represents a radical shift in perspective. It removes the 'problem' from the impaired individual and places it firmly with the way society is organised. It highlights the social and individual attitudes and behaviours that produce the physical and conceptual barriers that oppress disabled people. The social model has been emancipatory: it focuses upon the dismantling of barriers and grants individuals the power and responsibility to make decisions about their future. It also emphasises that current representations of disabled people as 'other', tragic or helpless victims are learned prejudices rather than rational responses. Morris (1992) highlights the role played by 'rights' in the social model: 'Our vision is of a society which recognizes our rights and our value as equal citizens rather than merely treating us as the recipient of other people's good will' (p. 10).

But this is not the last word. The social model has been criticised for reducing everything to economics, neglecting the stories and voices of disabled people and taking little account of physical experience of living with the kinds of impairments that cannot be solved by social manipulation. The social and medical models have been diametrically opposed in the way that they see disability and some suggest that placing lived experiences of people with disabilities back in the picture risks reinforcing a 'medical tragedy' perspective. However, the voice of disabled people is increasingly being heard.

A further 'affirmative' model (Swain and French, 2000) has emerged, inspired in particular by the Disability Arts Movement. This offers a positive identity, focusing upon the benefits of lifestyle and experience of being impaired, and challenges notions of 'normality and otherness'. It promotes the building of a positive collective identity through membership of campaigning groups such as the Disabled People's Movement. In common with other affirmative models, such as Black Power, it can be expressed by the slogan 'proud, angry and strong' (ibid, p. 573).

POINTS TO CONSIDER

- *What parallels can you draw between disability and ethnicity, gender and class?*

- *Do you agree with Mortimore that the* medical model *of disability has dominated educational discourses?*

- *To what extent have earlier cultural representations of disability and mental illness, as outlined in the extract, disappeared/transformed in contemporary media?*

- *What are the main implications for education of a shift from* medical, *to social and* affirmative *models of disability?*

The shift away from individualised and medicalised models has clearly been advantageous for people with disabilities. An emphasis on the social, cultural and economic barriers that construct disability has resulted in policies and practices that have made education, the workplace and leisure settings increasingly accessible. Yet some commentators have argued that the social model has more readily been applied to people with physical disabilities and sensory impairments than to people with 'learning difficulties' – the latter tending to be focused around individual deficiencies rather than on the ways that policies and practices construct those difficulties (Chappell, Goodley and Lawthorn, 2001).

Special or mainstream educational provision?

In 1970, legislation was introduced that meant that all children, irrespective of their disability, had an absolute right to education – it brought to an end the notion of the *ineducable child*. Mary Warnock chaired a committee asked to examine special education and, in 1978, the Warnock Report was published – it proved to be a landmark in special education provision. The terms 'special educational needs' and 'children with learning difficulties' were coined, using educational rather than medical criteria and placing the focus on appropriate provision rather than on conditions and treatments. The central recommendation was for the *integration* of the majority of children who were hitherto segregated.

The Warnock Report identified three main types of integration, namely:

- *locational integration* – children with special educational needs positioned in special units or classes on mainstream school sites;

- *social integration* – pupils in these special units or classes socialising with mainstream pupils during lunch and break times;

- *functional integration* – children with special educational needs taught for some or all of their time in mainstream classes.

More than 30 years after many of her recommendations were enshrined in law, Warnock publically reflected on the implementation of her ideas. The second extract illustrates her chief anxieties, especially with the application of the 'statementing' process.

EXTRACT TWO

Warnock, M (2005) Special Educational Needs: A New Look. *Philosophy of Education Society of Great Britain, pages 12–15*

The 1972 Education Act gave all children a right to education, however severe their disabilities. The concept of the ineducable child was abolished, and new principles of universal education were needed. The Committee of Inquiry into the Education of Handicapped Children and Young People was set up in 1974 with a view to establishing such principles, and its conclusions formed the basis of the Education Act 1981. I was chairman of this committee and I believe that, more than thirty years on, it is time for a radical review.

Special needs education, along with the pivotal concept of the statement of special educational need, has recently been subjected to serious criticism. Much of it is justified, and I would go further in this direction than many critics. In particular I would challenge the widely held view that, for all the problems in special needs education today, the statement should be retained as a 'safety net'. There is in my view a crucial lack of clarity in the concept of a statement, and while this continues to be so it is all but useless as a safety net. This lack of clarity was two aspects, one related to the concept of need, the other related to the concept of inclusion.

The statement of special educational need was seen in contrast to the medical model, according to which some children are 'normal', others are 'handicapped'. Our idea was that there are common educational goals – independence, enjoyment and understanding – towards which all children, irrespective of their abilities or disabilities should aim. We suggested that for some children the path towards these goals was smooth and easy, whereas for others it was beset by obstacles. They encountered special difficulties on the path towards the common goals. Every human being has certain needs and difficulties, so this approach was inclusive rather than exclusive.

Statements conferred a right to special provision on the children who received them, and imposed a corresponding duty on their local authorities to provide it. This was well and good, except that the criteria for deciding who should have a statement were never clear. The concept of need covers a wide spectrum: we say that a person who is severely dehydrated needs water, and also that a person whose car has broken down needs a new one. Whereas it was clear that severely disabled children needed special help, this was less clear with some of the milder disabilities, which might nevertheless prevent a child from learning successfully unless help was forthcoming. The lack of clarity was reflected in the fact that our original guess of how many children would receive statements was wildly off the mark. We thought the figure would be around 2%. The actual figure was around 20%.

Not only is there a gradation of needs which our early thinking did not adequately address, there is also a wide range of different kinds of need covered by the statement. Some needs (those of dyslexic children, for example) could usually be successfully met in mainstream classrooms. Others (those of children with autistic disorders or behavioural problems) were hard, if not impossible, to meet in this way. The conception of inclusion was taking a foothold in society generally. This meant that there was a tendency to overlook the differences not only between the educationally 'needy' and others, but also between various kinds of educational need.

The issue of mainstream versus special education is crucial. The inclusive ideology came to mean that, not only did statemented children have a right to special provision, they also had a right to be 'included' in mainstream schools, provided that they did not adversely affect the learning of others. This last proviso has been highly problematic, since an adverse effect on learning can be hard to prove. Since 2002, heads and governors have been liable to a criminal charge if they exclude a disruptive child from a mainstream school against the wishes of the parent. Yet it seems clear that disruptive children frequently hinder teaching and learning.

Special needs expert, Alan Dyson, has argued that there is a fundamental contradiction in the UK educational system between 'an intention to treat all learners as essentially the same and an equal and opposite intention to treat them as different' (Dyson 2001). I believe that he is right, and this means that, at the heart of our thinking about education, there is a confusion of which children are the causalities. The desire to 'include' children in single institutions is a desire to treat them as the same, and though this is a worthy ideal, it can be carried too far. For children are also different, and it is essential to acknowledge this, since refusal to address genuine differences can wholly undermine our attempts to meet children's needs. This, I believe, is what we are seeing today, and the way forward is for the government to set up another commission to review the situation.

One possibility would be the setting up of special (or 'specialist') schools based on a new concept of inclusion. Instead of the simplistic ideal of including all children 'under the same roof', we should consider the ideal of including all children in the common educational enterprise of learning, wherever they can learn best. There are some needs (for example, those of children suffering from autism and those of many children in care) which are more effectively met in separate institutions where the children are well known by their teachers and are not as vulnerable to bullying as they inevitably are in mainstream schools. There is a case for setting up a kind of school that is small and caters not for children with the most severe disabilities, but for those whose disabilities prevent them from learning in the environment of a large school. Such schools could be respected centres of learning. They could specialise in subjects like the Performing Arts or IT, and be open to the wider community in the evenings or at weekends. Statements could then serve a new and important purpose, as a kind of passport of entry. In other words, a statement would confer a right to attend a specialist school, and because such schools would be attractive to the wider community, parents would come to seek entry for their children, who would be properly included within their school.

Indeed small specialist schools of the kind described would be inclusive in an important sense of the word for children who currently suffer from feelings of exclusion within mainstream schools. The concept of inclusion must embrace the feeling of belonging, since such a feeling appears to be necessary both for successful learning and for more general well-being. I believe that small specialist schools could engender this feeling for many children who now lack it; but hard evidence is needed to support this view. A new review of special needs provision would have the important function of collecting and analyzing such evidence.

POINTS TO CONSIDER

- *Why does Warnock believe it is time to review educational provision for children with special educational needs? Do you agree?*

- *What do you view as the main advantages and disadvantages of:*

  - *integrating children with special educational needs into mainstream schools?*

  - *developing the kinds of specialist schools that Warnock outlines in the extract?*

How do recent educational policies demonstrate a conflict between an intention to treat all learners as essentially the same and an equal and opposite intention to treat them as different (Dyson 2001)? Does this extend beyond special educational needs provision?

- *Do you think children defined as 'gifted and talented' have 'special educational needs'?*

- *How might smaller schools enable learners with diverse needs to be/feel included?*

- *Warnock identifies a central problem with the concepts of need and statement – that these generic terms encompass a wide variety and degree of learning needs. How might educational structures be more responsive to these diverse needs?*

Since the initial Warnock Report, the objective has shifted from integration to inclusion. As noted above, the intent of integration was, wherever possible, to place children with special educational needs into mainstream education – and this frequently meant in segregated settings within mainstream schools. With little compulsion for the school to make significant changes in provision, the child with SEN needed to adapt to the mainstream school. Over the last 20 years or so, a discourse of inclusion has signalled a shifting emphasis. Successive policies have placed an increasing requirement on schools to consider the quality of their provision and to develop structures, teaching approaches and support systems in order to respond to the needs of all children, in particular those with SEN.

An inclusive education?

In the first part of the twenty-first century, inclusion has been at the centre of educational policy. The Special Educational Needs and Disability Act (SENDA) came into force in 2001, compelling schools to make appropriate arrangements for the inclusion of all children – to make *reasonable adjustments* and meet *anticipatory duties* for children with special educational needs.

The National Curriculum sets out statutory requirements in three principles for an inclusive curriculum:

A. *Setting suitable learning challenges*

B. *Responding to pupils' diverse learning needs*

C. *Overcoming potential barriers to learning and assessment for individuals and groups of pupils.*

(QCDA, 2010)

In 2004 the government published *Removing Barriers to Achievement*, a strategy for promoting inclusion for children with SEN in every school, targeting early intervention and raising expectations and attainment, and developing partnerships between services (2004). This led to the establishment of the Inclusive Development Programme – a four-year plan (2008–11) of continuing professional development designed to increase the confidence and expertise of managers, teachers, special educational needs coordinators (SENCOs) and other support staff in mainstream schools (DCSF, 2010). In 2008, the Inclusion Development Programme focused on dyslexia and speech, language and communication needs (SLCN). In 2009, the focus was on autistic spectrum disorders (ASD), in 2010 on behavioural, emotional and social difficulties (BESD) and in 2011 on moderate learning difficulties (MLD).

The third extract looks at inclusion in the higher education context and considers barriers to and potential for inclusive assessment. It argues for a move away from reactive 'special arrangements' in favour of a more proactive, truly inclusive approach.

EXTRACT THREE

Waterfield, J, West, B & Parker, M (2006) "Supporting Inclusive Practice: Developing an Assessment Toolkit". In Adams, M. & Brown, S. (2006) Towards Inclusive Learning in Higher Education: Developing Curricular for Disabled Students. Abingdon: Routledge, pages 80–81, 93

In the past decade, the UK higher education sector has witnessed an increase in the number of disabled students applying for and studying on a wide range of courses. The Higher Education Statistical Agency (2004) return for 2002/3 indicates approximately 106,000 students, namely 5.39 per cent of the student population have declared impairments, although the statistics conceal the true measure of the population and the percentages in individual institutions and in particular disciplines as it is based on a method of self-disclosure by the individual disabled student.

Until very recently funding programmes aimed at improving policy and provision for disabled students placed a major emphasis upon the development of specialist support services. This may have provided the opportunity for good developmental practice but did not necessarily create sector consistency, or the development of strategic approaches to inclusive practice. The case for inclusiveness was well made by the Beattie Report which sought to 'translate the concept of Inclusiveness into action' (Beattie 1999, item 2.6). Since 2000, disability funding programmes in England have encouraged dialogue and innovation between disability services and academic departments, to support institutional change and academic developments (HEFCE 2002).

In addition, the advent of the UK Disability Discrimination Act (DDA) Part 4 (2002) and, more recently, the Disability Discrimination Act (2005) have placed a legislative imperative upon educational establishments to be proactive and to engage with disabled students as a 'positive duty' to eliminate discriminatory practice. This has provided the sector with an opportunity, as well as a requirement, to address the validity of current practice and to take a more inclusive approach to the teaching, learning and assessment of disabled students while maintaining academic and professionally prescribed standards.

However, there remains a gap between legislation and practice. To date, the higher education system reflects many of society's inequalities where 'participation in education continues to be focused on fitting people into what is already available' (Stuart 2002). As Barton (2003) asserts, 'inclusion is not about assimilation or accommodation of individuals into an essentially unchanged system of practice'. Instead it is about the 'transformation of those deep structural barriers to change'. To achieve this transformation, there is a need to focus on opening up a dialogue, exploring innovative practice and challenging resistance to the removal of those 'deep structural barriers'. The genesis for our research was a concern for equity for disabled students, but we have subsequently pursued its value for the wider diverse student population and the breadth of learning styles encompassed by learners with a range of cultural and educational experiences. Our shift of emphasis was a response to the results from our first-year baseline research that revealed student learning styles and learning experiences that we believed may have transferable lessons for other student groups. To ensure our research was robust and valid, we felt it imperative to explore the assessment experiences of non-disabled students. Contributing to a higher education culture which does not single out one discrete group of students but which seeks to develop procedures which value diversity is fundamental to equality and social inclusion.

Across the UK the extensive use of 'special examination arrangements' for disabled students is reactive practice which is indicative of an assimilation culture; it forces students to adopt a disability identity, which confers on them a medical model and, as a purely practical institutional level, is an ad hoc *response with resource and equity implications that are neither desirable nor sustainable.*

[...] Inclusive assessment is a complex and contentious issue, however, by exploring students' assessment experiences and understanding the applicability of assessment practice for measuring learning outcomes, it is possible to begin to move the process

forward for equitable change. As the project has developed, the research team has become increasingly aware that inclusive assessment does not have to represent new methods of assessment and increased academic workload, but instead a greater utilisation of existing methods, learning from other disciplines and disabled student experience. As Elton (2000) prosaically states: 'I cannot think of anything more unfair than to treat all students as if they are the same when they are so manifestly not.' Thus, in working to address disability we may appear to have been discussing the periphery when in fact it has led us to examine the central core of university activity. We recognise that there may always remain a small group who will require something different as a response to an individual set of circumstances, a 'special arrangement' or one-off alternative. However, we believe that institutions need to adopt a more inclusive practice where traditional methods of assessment must be examined to better serve disabled students, other non-traditional students and students with a range of learning styles and experiences – in fact, all students.

POINTS TO CONSIDER

- *How far can a commitment to inclusion be reconciled with the other main educational discourse of the contemporary period – the Standards Agenda of raised achievement, market forces, competition, performance indicators and league tables?*

- *Look at other significant educational policies of the early twenty-first century – including Early Years Foundation Stage, Every Child Matters, Success for All – how evident is an inclusion discourse in these documents?*

- *How far do you think existing assessment practices accommodate the diversity of the student population and the breadth of learning styles encompassed by learners with a range of cultural and educational experiences?*

- *What might inclusive assessment look like in practice and what do you see as the main advantages and disadvantages of an approach like this?*

- *How inclusive do you think the assessment is on your degree course?*

There is evidently a gap between inclusion policy and practice. Teachers raise concerns of a perceived lack of resourcing and planning, that they lack the expertise, training and skills to teach children with severe learning difficulties effectively, and of the potential for inclusive practices to impact negatively on other children in the classroom. But a *one size fits all* education model is increasingly difficult to defend. Schools need to become more responsive to the diverse needs of the pupils they teach. Practical difficulties are largely due to the *newness* of the project and the haste at which initiatives have been implemented. There remains work to be done to realise the ideal of an education system that values and accommodates all learners equally and an inclusive society that celebrates the diversity of all the people that constitute it.

C H A P T E R   S U M M A R Y

As this chapter has demonstrated, educational provision for children with special educational needs has come a long way in a relatively short period of time. Mortimore outlined how specialist provision, based on a medical model of disability, was substituted with a social model and a drive to integrate SEN children into mainstream educational settings. Key figures, like Mary Warnock in the second extract, have questioned the extent that specific needs can be met within mainstream settings. Recently, as the third extract discusses, the spotlight has turned to inclusive education – placing an emphasis on schools to adapt to the diverse needs of all learners and extending beyond special educational needs to include other marginalised groups in society.

REFERENCES

Chappell, A, Goodley, D and Lawthorn, R (2001) 'Making connections: the relevance of the social model of disability for people with learning difficulties'. *British Journal of Learning Disabilities*, 29 (2), pp45–50

DCSF (2009) *Special educational needs in England, January 2008*. London: Department of Children Schools and Families

DCSF (2010) *Inclusion development programme* **http://nationalstrategies.standards.dcsf.gov.uk/ node/116691**

DFES (2004) *Removing barriers to achievement: the government's strategy for SEN*. London: Department for Education and Skills

Dyson, A (2001) 'Special needs in the twenty-first century: where we've been and where we're going', *British Journal of Special Education* 28(1), pp.24–29

QCDA (2010) *National curriculum inclusion statement*

Warnock, M (1978) *The Warnock report: special educational needs.* London: Her Majesty's Stationery Office

FURTHER READING

Cline, T and Frederickson, N (2009) *Special educational needs, inclusion and diversity* (2nd edition). Maidenhead: Open University Press

Hodkinson, A and Vickerman, P (2009) *Key issues in special educational needs and inclusion (Education Studies: Key Issues)* London: Sage

Westwood, P (2007) *Commonsense methods for children with special educational needs* (Fifth edition) London: Routledge

WEBSITES

http://nationalstrategies.standards.dcsf.gov.uk/inclusion

www.csie.org.uk/ – Centre for Studies on Inclusive Education

www.allfie.org.uk/index.html – The Alliance for Inclusive Education

www.education.gov.uk – New Department for Education

Theme three

Learning in the twenty-first century

Chapter 9
Education and globalisation

OBJECTIVES

By the end of this chapter you should have:
- identified some of the key features and key understandings of globalisation and considered their significance for education and learning;
- reflected critically upon the educational challenges and/or opportunities that globalisation is seen to pose;
- considered the roles that schools and universities could or should perform in educating citizens of the world.

Introduction

In recent years, the phenomenon – or set of phenomena – known widely as globalisation has attracted considerable attention from across the academic social sciences and in popular discussion and debate. However, relatively little attention has been afforded to relationships between education and globalisation, either to the impacts for schools and universities of what appears to be the increasing interconnection of the world, or to the role of education systems in *globalising* knowledge, information, cultural values and ideas (Dale and Roberts on, 2003).

This chapter begins by exploring some of the most influential explanations of how and why globalisation takes place. The first reading then draws attention to a number of key educational implications of these arguments. The second and third readings provide contrasting perspectives on the theory and experience of globalisation *from above* and *from below* and draw attention to the inequalities of power and diversity of experience which can often be ignored or neglected by over-simplistic or one-sided accounts.

A shrinking world?

> *The world is shrinking – or so it seems. At the end of the twentieth century, distances are not what they used to be.*

> (Allen and Hamnett, 1995, page 1)

Allen and Hamnett are not alone in their assertion that the world appears to be shrinking. From the late 1980s onwards, a growing chorus of academics and other commentators have argued that profound changes in the economic, social and political organisation of human activity have altered our understanding of the world. Technological innovation in networks of transport and communication has overcome many of the obstacles of physical space. Flows of international finance, of goods for sale and of people and ideas now move ever faster and more freely across the globe. Notions of *near* and *far* are challenged and rethought as people's relationships become stretched across space and as individuals become more and more aware of life beyond their own back door. As Allen and Hamnett continue: *True, fifty miles is still fifty miles if you pace it out, but our ability to cross such distances has altered greatly and so too has our notion of just how far is fifty miles* (Allen and Hamnett, 1995, page 1).

A very brief history of globalisation theory

As early as the late 1960s, geographer Donald Janelle observed that improvements in transport technology meant spatial distances between human settlements had become less and less significant as different places were brought ever closer together through reduced travel time (Janelle, 1969). He famously described that the Scottish and English capital cities, Edinburgh and London, had *converged* at a rate of thirty minutes per year over two hundred years: in 1776 the journey could only be made over four days by stage-coach whereas by 1969, when Janelle was writing, the distance could be covered in just three hours by aeroplane. Of course, the physical distance between the two places remains exactly the same but the perceived and practical distance is remarkably changed. This in turn alters the options available to people and the choices that they make. Consider how many undergraduate students today choose to leave their hometowns to go to university. Do you think quite as many would do so if it was going to take them four whole days to visit family or friends during their holidays?

Likewise, developments in communication technology have played an enormously significant role in collapsing spatial distance: compare an email sent and received today almost instantaneously anywhere in the world with a telegram message sent over land and/or sea at the turn of the century. Also during the 1960s, the media scholar Marshall McLuhan introduced the concept of *the global village* arguing that advanced communications technology had provided an extended *electronic nervous system* whereby the radio and telephone become our long-distance ears and television and the internet our long-distance eyes. For McLuhan, the whole world had become a village because people now witnessed firsthand (albeit remotely) the consequences or their actions on a global scale and would therefore become more aware of their responsibilities to other people. (McLuhan, 1964)

The *stretching* of human interactions over increasingly great distances has also been theorised by sociologist Anthony Giddens using the term *time-space distanciation* (Giddens, 1990). Giddens argues that in early human societies, it was generally necessary for people to be in the same place at the same time as each other in order to exchange goods, share information or to build relationships. Notions of time, space and action were closely bound together: people met in certain places at certain times to do specific things. Today we can – and often have to – interact with people *remotely* and actions need no longer be embedded in specific locations: video-conferencing allows boardroom meetings to be held with multiple participants in different countries, wi-fi and internet technology allows your garden to become your office or your bedroom your high street shop. In this way, many activities have become *deterritorialised* or footloose – they can happen in variety of different places and at any time.

POINTS TO CONSIDER

- *Can you see any implications for education in Janelle's, McLuhan's or Giddens' ideas?*

- *How accurate do you think McLuhan's metaphor of the global village is? How much do you think people care about others living several thousand miles away? And how responsible for those others do you think most people feel? Can you identify any obstacles in the way of a global sense of community?*

You may already have considered that both the processes of *convergence* and *distanciation* have in fact been happening to a greater or lesser extent for quite some time: by the mid-nineteenth century, Janelle's journey between Edinburgh and London was already possible within just ten hours by steam train. In fact, one of the key areas of disagreement within globalisation theory is when the process actually began (see for example, Held and McGrew, 2001). Does the term refer to a distinct, recent phenomenon? Or is it the continuation of already existing historical trends? The majority of commentators concur that, at the very least, the last three or four decades have witnessed a dramatic acceleration of existing processes.

In 1989, the geographer David Harvey offered a very influential analysis, drawn from a Marxist perspective which saw free-market capitalism as the principal motor of globalisation and the global oil-crisis and stock-exchange collapse of 1973 as an important turning point. Up until then, Fordism – named after the American car manufacturer Henry Ford – had become the dominant industrial and economic model across much of the Western world. Fordist economies were characterised by mass, assembly-line production of consumer goods for a mass domestic market. Fixed organisational structures with clear divisions of labour and firm national boundaries were important here. In order to ensure efficient mass production, individual workers performed very specific limited roles and in order to ensure mass consumption, industry worked closely with national government to ensure that the domestic market was protected from foreign competition and the national population was sufficiently well looked after to be able to buy new refrigerators, new television-sets and new cars (Brown and Lauder, 1997).

However, from 1973 onwards, things began to change. As national economies began to flail, new ways of creating profit were sought. Rigid structures and tight government regulation now came to be seen as obstacles rather than safeguards: greater flexibility and increased scope for competition was required. For Harvey, it is the *logic of capital* as it tries to find ways to maximise profit, minimise cost and maximise its market that has driven globalisation. *National* governments, *national* markets and *national* labour forces are no longer the primary concern of *international* industry and finance. It is now much easier, faster and cheaper to transport all manner of component parts or end products around the globe while electronic banking and the proliferation of plastic money have simultaneously permitted the freer flow of finance. Markets now expand outside of national borders and are stimulated by the creation of demand for ephemeral fashions or trends.

But globalisation is not a phenomenon confined to the realm of global economics. All of these changes have significant political, cultural and, as we shall go on to discuss, educational impact too. As new forms of organisation are now able to locate and trade almost anywhere in the world, potential sites are forced to compete for business. In this way, the legitimacy of national governments can be challenged as they are pulled between their responsibilities for the welfare of their populations and the demands of international capital. Increasingly, *inter*national, or *trans*national organisations such as the European Union, United Nations, International Monetary Fund or World Bank offer an alternative framework of authority or influence.

In the social and/or cultural sphere, people and ideas once represented as distant or foreign become ever more familiar and close: city centre restaurants and supermarket aisles now regularly showcase international cuisine; television documentaries and satellite link-ups bring international news as it happens into your living room; through choice and necessity, people migrate in their millions across international borders and local communities become increasingly multicultural. For Harvey, the constant flux and uncertainty of international finance, industry, commodities, images, people and ideas creates a maelstrom or tumultuous whirlpool of modern day living which has potentially disorienting effects. In this light, recent resurgences of nationalist politics, the growing significance of xenophobically defended exclusive communities, or the search for historical roots and the growing attractions of the heritage industry, can be understood as a response to a perceived turmoil – an attempt to find a secure footing where everything is change. This last point illustrates one further important feature of contemporary globalisation: it is complex and can have apparently contradictory effects. For example, while McLuhan saw the future in terms of a *global village* of shared responsibility and interconnection, Harvey sees fragmentation, hostility and mutual suspicion as groups and individuals are forced to compete.

Globalising education?

But what does any of this mean for education? The last ten years have witnessed an awakening of interest in this important area (see for example, Dale and Robertson, 2003; Suarez-Orozco and Qin-Hilliard, 2004). Taken from the introduction to their edited collection, *Globalisation and Education: Critical Perspectives*, in the extract below Burbules and Torres summarise what they regard as some of the key consequences of globalisation for educational policy in terms of economic, political and cultural impact.

Burbules, NC and Torres, CA (2000) Globalisation and Education: An Introduction in NC Burbules and CA Torres (Eds) Globalisation and Education: Critical Perspectives. London: Routledge, pages 19–23

EXTRACT ONE

At the economic level, because globalization affects employment, it touches upon one of the primary traditional goals of education: preparation for work. Schools will need to reconsider this mission in light of changing job markets in a post-Fordist work environment; new skills and the flexibility to adapt to changing job demands and, for that matter, changing jobs during a lifetime; and dealing with an increasingly competitive international labor pool. Yet, schools are not only concerned with preparing students as producers; increasingly, schools help shape consumer attitudes and practices as well, as encouraged by the corporate sponsorship of educational institutions and of products, both curricular and extracurricular, that confront students every day in their classrooms. This increasing commercialization of the school environment has become remarkably bold and explicit in its intentions (as in the case of Chris Whittle's project, Channel One, [. . .] which admits quite openly that it offers schools free televisions so as to expose children to a force-fed diet of commercials in their classrooms every day).

The broader economic effects of globalization tend to force national educational policies into a neoliberal framework that emphasizes lower taxes; shrinking the states sector and "doing more with less"; promoting market approaches to school choice (particularly vouchers); rational management of school organizations' performance assessment (testing); and deregulation in order to encourage new providers (including on-line providers) of educational services.

At the political level, a repeated point here has been the constraint on national/state policy making posed by external demands from transnational institutions. Yet, at the same time that economic coordination and exchange have become increasingly well regulated, and as stronger institutions emerge to regulate global economic activity, with globalization there has also been a growing internationalization of global conflict, crime, terrorism, and environmental issues, but with an inadequate development of political institutions to address them. Here, again, educational institutions may have a crucial role to play in addressing these problems, and the complex network of intended and unintended human consequences that have followed from the growth of global corporations, global mobility, global communication, and global expansion. In part, this awareness may help to foster a more critical conception of what education for 'world citizenship' requires.

Finally, global changes in culture deeply affect educational policies, practices, and institutions. Particularly in advanced industrial societies, for instance, the question of 'multiculturalism' takes on special meaning in a global context. How does the discourse of liberal pluralism – which has been the dominant framework for multicultural education in developed societies learning to live with others within a compact of mutual tolerance and respect – extend to a global order in which the gulf of differences becomes wider, the sense of interdependence and common interest more attenuated, and the grounding

EXTRACT ONE continued

of affiliation more abstract and indirect (if it exists at all)? With the growing global pressures on local cultures, is it education's job to help preserve them? How should education prepare students to deal with the terms of local, regional, national, and transnational conflict, as cultures and traditions whose histories of antagonism may have been held partly in suspension by strong, overarching nation-states break loose when those institutions lose some of their power and legitimacy? To the degree that education can help support the evolving construction of the self and, at a more general level, the constitution of identities, how can multiculturalism as a social movement, as citizenship education, and as an antiracist philosophy in curriculum intervene in the dynamics of social conflict emerging between global transformations and local responses?

POINTS TO CONSIDER

- *The extract identifies preparation for employment as one primary goal of education. Can you think of particular jobs typical of Fordist and post-Fordist economies? How might schools or universities help prepare students for each?*

- *Can you think of examples of how a neoliberal framework may have impacted educational policy and practice in your own country?*

- *The authors suggest that educational institutions may have a critical role to play in addressing problems such as global conflict, terrorism and environmental risk. Do you agree? How might they perform this role?*

- *Throughout the extract, the authors seem most concerned to highlight educational challenges or potential obstacles posed by globalisation. Can you suggest any comparable opportunities?*

The experience of globalisation from above and from below

Torres and Burbules pose some important and interesting questions. Try to keep these in mind as you continue to read. Torres and Burbules, and Harvey before them, write primarily of the dangers, challenges and tensions wrought by globalisation. In other – often very powerful – accounts, globalisation is presented in terms of remarkable innovation and fantastic opportunity. Many politicians, economists and other commentators have, for example, celebrated the supposed freedom of movement of goods and people and ideas suggesting we now live in a borderless world. Yet it does not take much reflection to recognise that the world is not everyone's oyster, playground or market-place. Critically, the effects of globalisation – both its opportunities and challenges – are experienced by different people in different ways.

A regular criticism of early globalisation theorists – including McLuhan, Giddens and Harvey – is that they offer only a partial point of view. Many accounts are charged with

Western- or Euro-centrism. For if the world does in fact appear to be shrinking, *it is not shrinking for everyone in all locations* in the same manner or at the same rate (Allen and Hamnett, 1995, page 1). Massey (1995), for example, calls for greater attention to be paid to the complex networks of power in which people have historically been positioned, both across the globe and within each local community and which mediate the experience of change. Despite the intensified development of transport and communication elsewhere, large tracts of the globe remain *quite literally off all kinds of maps – maps of telecommunications, maps of world trade and finance, maps of global tourism and the like* (Allen and Hamnett, 1995, page 1.) and this is important to recognise.

Harvey's contention that the *maelstrom* of everyday globalised living is a distinctly new phenomenon can also be criticised. While sections of today's British public may feel that in recent years their country has been invaded by foreign multinational corporations, American popular culture or immigrant labour, what is so new about this? As a consequence of Europe's first voyages of discovery in the fifteenth century and later empire building and colonial conquest, *it is a feeling which has been known for many centuries in many parts of the globe* (Massey, 1995, page 52).

Many of these criticisms can be addressed if we pay attention not only to overarching global trends and the actions and decisions of key players such as international financiers and the political community but also to the agency and possible resistance of local communities, that is, the experience of globalisation, *from below*.

Globalising *through* education?

There is one other important dimension that is missing from Torres and Burbules' summary as it is presented above. Not only is education impacted upon *by* globalisation but educational institutions are themselves important vehicles *for* globalising particular forms of knowledge, values and ideas. This perspective is examined in both readings 2 and 3.

In extract two, Joel Spring describes the importance given to education by one of the most powerful contemporary international institutions, the World Bank, and considers some of its effects. As Spring explains, *the World Bank is the leading global investor in education and is linked through extensive networks to other worldwide organisations. Through these networks the Bank is a major participant in global discourses about education* (2009, page 29). The World Bank provides educational loans to developing countries because it believes that education is the key to economic success. However, loans are given on the understanding that national governments will implement any necessary adjustments to existing provision so that school systems fall in line with the Bank's own vision of appropriate educational structures and priorities. Currently the World Bank believes that *the ability of society to produce, select, adapt, commercialise, and use knowledge is critical for sustained economic growth and improved living standards,* and that, *schools should be oriented in accord* (quoted in Spring, 2009, page 37).

If the World Bank represents a globalising force, *from above*, extract three is written from the perspective of those who experience the globalising effects of education *from below*. It challenges the idea that others – such as the World Bank – know best when it comes to education and asks us to reconsider what, and whose, forms of knowledge are most valuable or most appropriate in equipping learners to address the local *and global* challenges they may face today.

EXTRACT TWO

Spring, J (2009) Globalization of Education: An Introduction. *Abingdon: Routledge, pages 40–44*

The World Bank and the Ideal Personality for the Knowledge Economy

The World Bank's concept of the knowledge economy includes a particular idea about individuals' psychological attitudes and dispositions. A section of the World Bank report Lifelong Learning in the Global Knowledge Economy *contains a section with the descriptive title: 'Equipping Learners with the Skills and Competencies They Need to Succeed in a Knowledge Economy.' Two of the three competencies that are listed relate to psychological attitudes and dispositions. These competencies could require major changes in some of the world's cultures. For instance, the first listed competency is acting autonomously.*

> *Acting autonomously: Building and exercising a sense of self, making choices and acting in the context of a larger picture, being oriented toward the future, being aware of the environment, understanding how one fits in, exercising one's rights and responsibilities, determining and executing a life plan, and planning and carrying out personal projects. (World Bank, 2003:21)*

The goal of acting autonomously is echoed in the European Commission's 1998 White Paper on the knowledge economy: "The ultimate aim of education is to develop the autonomy of each person and of his/her professional capacity, to make of the person a privileged element of adaptation and evolution." (cited in Stoer and Magalhaes, 2004, page 325).

Cross-cultural psychologists associate the above character traits with individualist societies as contrasted with collectivist societies that emphasize acting in harmony with the group. Acting autonomously are not values of collectivist communities such as many Asian, Islamic, and Indigenous societies. In fact, the values that the World Bank are recommending instilling in children are those of a competitive marketplace that emphasise individual competition.

In other words, the World Bank is advocating changing the cultural values of many groups of peoples. Cross-cultural psychologist Harry C. Triandis identifies these contrasting character traits of individualist and collectivist societies in the table opposite (Triandis, 2001)

Overall, the United States, headquarters of the World Bank, is ranked as the most individualist nation in the world. Below is a global ranking of the ten most individualist nations (Oishi, 2000:100):

1 United States	*6 Norway*
2 Australia	*7 Italy*
3 Denmark	*8 Austria*
4 Germany	*9 Hungary*
5 Finland	*10 South Africa*

EXTRACT TWO *continued*

Table of individualist and collectivist personalities

Individualist	Collectivist
Hedonism, stimulation, self-direction	Tradition and conformity
Good opinion of self (self-enhancing)	Modest
Goals fit personal needs	Goals show concern with needs of others
Desire for individual distinctiveness	Desire for blending harmoniously with the group
Value success and achievement because it makes the individual look good	Value success and achievement because it reflects well on the group
More concerned with knowing one's feelings	Attuned to feelings of others and striving for interpersonal harmony
Exhibits 'social loafing' of 'gold-bricking' – trying to minimize work in group efforts	No social loafing in group efforts
Less sensitive to social rejection	More sensitive to social rejection
Less modest in social situations	More modest in social situations
Less likely to feel embarrassed	More likely to feel embarrassed

The ten most collectivist nations (beginning with the most collectivist) are:

1 China   6 Peru

2 Columbia   7 Ghana

3 Indonesia   8 Nepal

4 Pakistan   9 Nigeria

5 Korea   10 Tanzania

The second of the competencies, using tools interactively, includes skills needed for a knowledge economy by stressing the use of technological tools, information, and symbols.

> Using tools interactively: *Using tools as instruments for an active dialogue; being aware of and responding to the potential of new tools; and being able to use language, text, symbols information and knowledge and technology interactively to accomplish goals. (World Bank, 2003:22)*

These competencies would dramatically replace the reliance of indigenous cultures on traditional tools, ways of knowing, and oral traditions. From a culturalist perspective, local communities would probably adapt these tools to their culture. On the other hand, total acceptance of this package of tools and symbol usages combined with a stress on individualism might result in the transformation of many of the world's cultures.

The final competency implies a world of nomads; workers moving around the globe and having to adapt to multicultural workplaces. In this context, the knowledge economy becomes a world of migrant workers including corporate leaders, managers, technical operatives and professionals, skilled and unskilled labourers. The third competency focuses on social interaction.

> Functioning in socially heterogenous groups: *Being able to interact effectively with other people, including those from different backgrounds; recognizing the social embeddedness of individuals; creating social capital; and being able to relate well to others, cooperate, and manage and resolve conflict. (World Bank, 2003:22)*

Preparation for competencies in multicultural settings is indicated in learning to interact with 'those from different backgrounds' and 'recognizing the social embeddedness of others.' A phrase that at first glance might not be understood is 'creating social capital.'

> *By improving people's ability to function as members of their communities, education and training also increases social capital (broadly defined as social cohesion or social ties), thereby helping to build human capital, increase economic growth, and stimulate development. Social capital also improves education and health outcomes and child welfare, increases tolerance for gender and racial equity, enhances civil liberty and economic and civic equity, and decreases crime and tax evasion. (World Bank, 2003:3–4)*

As this quote indicates, social capital can be thought of as ethical or moral values that regulate the interactions, 'social cohesion or social ties,' of community members. A person with social capital will not commit criminal acts, 'decreases crime and tax evasion,' and will ensure the welfare of children and social justice. Of course, 'crime' and 'social justice' are relative concepts depending on the laws and customs of a particular nation or culture. For example, for many years it has been illegal for women in Saudi Arabia to drive automobiles (Fattah, 2007). Does this mean that social capital in Saudi Arabia would include supporting this law? On the other hand, increased social capital as stated above is supposed to lead to 'tolerance for gender and racial equity.' In this context, for better or worse, the World Bank's goal is to change the laws and customs of Saudi Arabia regarding women's driving through the use of education to increase social capital. While I would not dispute the idea that women should be allowed to drive, it cannot be denied that the World Bank's concept of social capital is designed to change the cultures and laws of societies and nations.

If the concept of social capital is integrated into the concept of human capital, then the goals of education broaden to fostering individualism, developing technical and language skills, learning to function in multicultural settings, and learning to be ethical or moral in relationship to others in the context of promoting civil liberty; racial, gender, and economic equity; and obedience to national laws.

In summary, the World Bank's ideal social personality for the knowledge economy is a person who acts autonomously and is focused on a sense of self. This concept of individualism, in contrast to personalities in collectivist societies, is a reflection of the values of nations like the United States. It is a personality ideally suited for individual competition in economic markets. In addition, the Bank's concept includes the ability to migrate between culture and work in multicultural settings. While focusing on her/his self, this type of personality also learns to be obedient to the laws and customs of a nation. The focus on individualism raises the important question: Is the World Bank practicing a form of cultural imperialism?

POINTS TO CONSIDER

- *In extract one, Torres and Burbules asked, with the growing global pressures on local cultures, is it education's job to help preserve them? From this reading, what do you think would be the World Bank's reply?*

- *Can you defend their position? Should the World Bank – or any other external organisation – aim to change the Saudi Arabian laws on women driving? If so, how? And is education an appropriate tool?*

- *How successful do you think your own national education system is in preparing learners for the knowledge economy (as prescribed by the World Bank)?*

- *The European Commission are reported as stating that the ultimate aim of education is to develop individual autonomy. Do you agree?*

EXTRACT THREE

Burford, G, Ngila, LO and Rafiki, Y (2003) 'Education, indigenous knowledge and globalisation' in Science in Africa *March 2003. Online magazine available at: www.scienceinafrica.co.za/2003/march/ik.htm*

The majority of African youth still subscribe to the 'American dream', and on a smaller scale, to the 'urban dream'. The growing trend towards urbanisation is encouraging thousands to abandon their indigenous knowledge, in the belief that new knowledge and new opportunities are to be found in town. Yet the realities of mass unemployment, the high costs of urban life and of further education, and the growing pandemic of AIDS testify that this is not the case. Many end up homeless, jobless and penniless, with neither the traditional skills that sustained their ancestors nor the specialised and expensive skills required for employment in a modern town. The inevitable result is poverty.

The enormity of the threat posed by the break-up of indigenous communities has not yet been fully realised by many of those now in power, although it has always been obvious to community elders. Many mistakenly believe that the reason that rural African societies have not evolved in the same way as the 'civilised' west is a lack of knowledge. In truth, it has been a matter of free choice to protect the natural environment and to maintain traditional lifestyles. The culture and traditions that form an integral part of indigenous knowledge provide codes of conduct addressing all aspects of the community – economic, social, environmental and psychological. When they are in place, they keep the society in its equilibrium.

It is widely assumed that poverty is an unavoidable consequence of climate change such as drought. For centuries, however, indigenous knowledge has provided Africa's tribal peoples with practical solutions to the problems of a fluctuating climate. As an example, the Maasai pastoralists of northern Tanzania and southern Kenya traditionally know where to find water, and green shrubs that can be fed to young calves, even during long periods of drought. Likewise, in Ethiopia, often regarded as inevitably dependent on Western aid, the threat of famine can be overcome by local expertise, as Worede (in Seabrook, 1993:31) explains:

135

'There is a wild plant that grows on the Somali border, under the driest conditions, less than 200 mm of rain a year... There are other crops, things people have known where to find in distress times. They go to the mountains and pick them and survive somehow. But if you destroy the natural environment of such plants, you lose these resources, and your monocultures won't save you.'

In our opinion, the greatest threat to the economic stability of the African continent is not its changing climate. Rather, it is the gradual erosion of indigenous knowledge and the accompanying destruction of natural wealth – plants, animals, insects, soils, clean air and water – and human cultural wealth, such as songs, proverbs, folklore and social co-operation. This robs people of their ability to respond to social and environmental change, both by removing the resource base, and by attacking the foundations of human identity.

There are many fashionable phrases currently popular with international agencies – sustainable development, conflict resolution, good governance, poverty alleviation, environmental stewardship – which could all be translated as 'fostering a sense of peace with ourselves and our cultural identity'. It is never easy for the oppressed to become anything other than oppressors, but we believe that it can be achieved through rebuilding the sense of self-esteem and confidence that colonialism and the global market have sought to eliminate. This does not mean a return to the destructive tribalism, grounded in insecurity and fear, which has haunted so many countries in Africa. Rather, in order to live on good terms with the neighbours – local and international, human and non-human – with whom we share this planet, we must first rediscover an awareness of who we are. At the same time, we belong to a tribe, to a nation, and to the world.

The real meaning of education: 'bringing up and drawing out'

The English word 'education' is often taken to refer to the formal systems of schooling originally introduced to Africa by colonial administrators, and further developed by post-independence governments. An examination of its original meaning, however, reveals something quite different. Senge (1990) highlights the fact that education is derived from two Latin words: educare, 'to rear or foster', and educere, 'to draw out or develop'. Education thus incorporates all the processes of raising up young people to adulthood, and drawing out or developing their potential to contribute to society, that are traditionally found in rural communities. Learning to hunt wild game or herd livestock, prepare food or weave cloth, search for wild honey or distinguish medicinal plants from poisonous ones, is arguably closer to the true meaning of 'education' than learning to make and interpret marks on paper.

This should not be interpreted as meaning that literacy, numeracy and the acquisition of new languages are unnecessary. No society can exist in isolation: people have always sought ways to communicate with one another and to trade in goods and services, and this has never been more important than it is today. In an increasingly interdependent world, it is as essential for us to be fluent in the languages of international economics and politics – in order to defend our rights and demand development on our own terms – as in the languages of animal tracks, bird calls and weather patterns.

EXTRACT THREE *continued*

What is currently missing, in most societies, is a system of teaching and learning that can combine the two. African children are either kept in their home environments, missing out on the 'modern' aspects of education, or (increasingly) forced into full-time formal schooling, missing out on the 'traditional'. The latter often furthers the neo-colonial mentality by building aspirations of urban life and encouraging young people to believe that they have no future in rural communities.

POINTS TO CONSIDER

- *Again, how do you think these writers would reply to Torres and Burbules' question, should education help preserve local cultures? Why?*

- *What is your own point of view?*

- *The authors suggest that the erosion of indigenous knowledge risks economic instability and environmental destruction. What other consequences might there be?*

- *The authors also suggest that education should help foster a sense of peace with ourselves and our cultural identity. How successful in this respect is educational policy and practice in your own country?*

The previous two extracts illustrate that, not only is education impacted upon by globalisation but it is itself a vehicle for globalising knowledge, values and ideas. This raises difficult yet important questions concerning what forms of knowledge – and *whose* forms of knowledge – are valued and in what context: education can be used as both a powerful tool for cultural stabilisation/preservation *and* as a motor for cultural change. It seems unlikely that either an absolute insistence on the preservation of tradition or an absolute insistence on the necessity of change will provide us with the most useful solutions to contemporary challenges. However, it is important to examine and question the globalised networks of power that both operate and can be resisted through education: who determines the pace and direction of change and by what rationale?

C H A P T E R   S U M M A R Y

This chapter has described that globalisation refers to a complex and contradictory set of processes which can have profound economic, political and socio-cultural effects. It then described some of the key implications for education emphasising that processes of globalisation are experienced, interpreted, embraced and/or resisted by different people in different ways.

REFERENCES

Allen, J and Hamnett, C (eds) (1995) *A Shrinking World? Global Unevenness and Inequality*. London: Open University Press

Brown, P and Lauder, H 'Education, Globalization and Economic Development' in Halsey, AH, Lauder H, Brown, P and Wells, AS (eds) (1997) *Education: Culture, Economy, and Society*. Oxford: Oxford University Press

Dale, R and Robertson, SL (2003) 'Editorial. Introduction', *Globalisation, Societies and Education* 1(1), pp3–11

Giddens, A (1990) *The Consequences of Modernity*. Cambridge: Polity Press

Harvey, D (1989) *The Conditions of Postmodernity: An Enquiry into the Origins of Cultural Change*. Oxford: Blackwell

Janelle, DG (1969) 'Spatial reorganisation: a model and concept', *Annals of the American Association of Geographers* 59, pp348–64

McLuhan, M (1964) *Understanding Media: The Extensions of Man*. New York: McGraw Hill

Massey, D (1995) *A Place in the World? Places, Culture and Globalisation*. London: Open University Press

Suarez-Orozco, M and Qin-Hilliard, DB (eds.) (2004) *Globalization: Culture and Education in the New Millenium*. Berkeley: University of California Press

World Bank (2003) *Lifelong Learning in the Global Knowledge Economy*. Washington: The International Bank for Reconstruction and Development /The World Bank

FURTHER READING

Apple, M, Kenway, J and Singh, M (eds.) (2005) *Globalizing Education: Policies, Pedagogies and Politics*. New York: Peter Lang

Lauder, H, Brown, P, Dillabough, J and Halsey, HA (eds.) (2006) *Education, Globalization and Social Change*. Oxford: Oxford University Press

Orr, D (2004) *Earth in Mind: On Education, Environment, and the Human Prospect*. Washington DC: First Island Press

WEBSITES

www.worldbank.org/education

www.polity.co.uk/global/ – This website accompanies the Global Transformations book series and offers useful additional resources and web links

www.globalteacher.org.uk/global_ed.htm – This website offers advice and information for teachers keen to explore issues of globalisation and introduce global perspectives within their schools

Chapter 10
Learning in a digital age

OBJECTIVES

By the end of this chapter you should have:
- considered how developments in technology impact on the lives of children and young people;
- reflected on the opportunities and risks that arise from the rapid expansion of internet use;
- understood and reflected on emerging themes in the use of technology in education;
- evaluated the potential of Web 2.0 technologies for learning and teaching.

The chapter considers the extent that technological advancements impact on learning and teaching. It reflects on the capacity of recent developments to provide new and exciting opportunities for learner and teacher engagement, as well as the new threats that emerge. The extracts reflect current academic interest in the pedagogic potential of the internet and of Web 2.0 technologies in particular, and on the uses and misuses of technology in the classroom.

Introduction

It is hard to imagine a world without mobile phones, digital cameras, portable computers and the internet. Yet all of these technological developments are remarkably new. None of them existed in recognisable form prior to the 1990s and their widespread availability and use is later still. Even technologies that have come to prominence in the twenty-first century (such as MP3 players, DVD recorders, Freeview TV, wireless internet, GPS handheld devices, touch screens and 3G networks) seem far from novel today. Arguably these technologies, and the speed at which they develop, have become the defining characteristic of the contemporary period. They have combined to make a radically different world from the one that existed even 20 years ago – think about how different your life would be without your mobile phone!

The school-age children and young people of the 2010s will not be conscious of a world predating these technologies. Notwithstanding significant inequalities in terms of access to resources, the use of digital equipment, computers and internet is largely intuitive and natural to them. Contrast this with adults in their 30s and beyond who have lived through this period of rapid change.

Marc Prensky famously distinguished between what he called *digital natives* and *digital immigrants* (2001). He claimed that young people who have grown up in the *digital age* (the *natives*) have acquired an entirely new way of thinking, communicating and processing information. Conversely, *immigrants* have to learn a new language and struggle to detach from the way they were socialised to think and communicate. The central concern, from Prensky's perspective, is that in the early stages of the twenty-first century, the *immigrants* are charged with teaching the *natives* – and that this disjuncture is bad news. He argued that *the single biggest problem facing education today is that our Digital Immigrant instructors, who speak an outdated language (that of the pre-digital age), are struggling to teach a population that speaks an entirely new language.* (Prensky, 2001, page 2).

You might be inclined to agree with Prensky – it is certainly worth reading his short and forceful paper and you can access easily online (particularly as you are probably a digital native!). His contentions have proved controversial, not least because he constructs a dichotomy that is far more complex in reality: in all likelihood you will have been taught by teachers who were entirely at ease with technology and others who were fearful, resistant and ignorant of the potential. Nevertheless, the notion that pupils *can be* more at ease with technology than their teachers raises key issues and questions: How might this impact on (power) relations between pupils and teachers? How might the relative discomfort of the teacher impact on her self-confidence and on curriculum development and delivery? How can teachers be encouraged and trained to make more efficient use of new technologies? Is it possible and/or desirable for pupils to teach their teachers about the digital world? How can teachers most effectively utilise the additional knowledge and skills their pupils possess? These questions frame reflection throughout this chapter.

Educational opportunities and threats of the internet

Arguably the most significant technological advancement in the modern world is the internet. And educational settings and relations have been particularly affected by its progress into our contemporary way of life. The internet has dramatically altered the methods of information access, retrieval, processing and presenting. It has also changed the nature of information – with multiple voices and perspectives available at the touch of a button. Whereas the undergraduate Education Studies student 15 years ago would have spent hours in the library sifting through books and paper journals, today you can access a wealth of information at your computer, via google scholar, google books, electronic journals or numerous less academic sources. Consequently, research and evidence-gathering activities are now much more about skills in managing electronic data and evaluating the credibility of sources.

So the emergence of the internet has transformed information processing. It has also changed the way we communicate with one another. The capacity to communicate more easily and quickly evidently changes the way people interact with one another. E-mail, in particular, has transformed communication and this has impacted on the way that teachers and pupils relate to one another. Very little non face-to-face communication took place between teachers and pupils prior to the advent of e-mail. Today, teachers and lecturers are far more accessible: young people expect to be able to contact their teachers and to receive replies promptly. Moreover, e-mail communications tend to be far more informal, without the constraints of letter-writing conventions. Think about how differently you write an e-mail compared with a written letter, how speedily you expect a response and how different this makes the interaction.

Today many teachers go beyond e-mail to make use of other internet-based means of communication. Courses appear in Virtual Learning Environments, making use of tools like blogs, wikis and discussion forums to aid communication. Some teachers encourage their students to make contact with them via social networking sites such as Facebook, Twitter, Bebo or MySpace. In fact, as you will see later in the chapter, informal educational settings are being established via these social networking sites, so that the classroom encounter between trained and certified teacher and the pupil as compulsory attendee are being bypassed.

POINTS TO CONSIDER

You have read about three ways that the internet spreads informality in education:

- *by providing access to a wide variety of evidence outside traditional, formal sources;*

- *through electronic communications (especially between teachers and pupils);*

- *through emerging digital educational sites outside of formal educational settings.*

  - *Can you think of an example of each of these instances?*

  - *What opportunities and threats emerge from the emergence of these informal educational settings?*

Educational and childhood experts have become fascinated with the potential the internet provides. Read the following extract, which identifies a number of the current hopes and fears. As you read the list at the end of the extract, consider how each point impacts on educational settings.

EXTRACT ONE

Livingstone, S (2009) Children and the Internet. *Cambridge: Polity, pages 28–30*

Great expectations abound regarding children and the internet. Optimists relish new opportunities for self-expression, sociability, community engagement, creativity and new literacies. For children, it is hoped that the internet can support new forms of learning, new ways of thinking even, and that it can overcome political apathy among the young. Pessimists foresee the expanded scope for state surveillance, commercial exploitation and harmful or criminal activities. For children, it is feared that the internet is introducing new risks and harms into their lives – commercial, sexual, ideological, abusive. The fears may dominate the newspaper headlines, and they are readily expressed by parents, teachers and children themselves. But it is the great expectations that are driving internet adoption and use at the level of government policy, commercial enterprise, community provision and domestic consumption.

Popular discourses tend to float freely above the everyday realities of children's internet experiences, occasionally acknowledging puzzled dismay that young people live in such a different world from the (nostalgically remembered) youth of today's adults. Too often they 'essentialize the child category, denying children's diversity and their status as social actors, and because they rest on technologically determinist understandings of ICT' (Holloway and Valentine, 2003:72; see also Buckingham, 2007a) .... without strong empirical findings moral panics readily take hold, as they have done many times before, catalyzing society's perennial anxieties about childhood and triggering media headlines, public anxieties and official inquiries. Throughout the twentieth century,

> *Each new media technology brought with it great promise for social and educational benefits, and great concern for children's exposure to inappropriate and harmful content. (Wartella and Jennings, 2000: 31)*

....Adopting the overarching lens of opportunities and threats, and setting aside for the moment the crucial issue of the relations and overlaps between them (though this will be a theme throughout this book), we may scope the agenda thus:

Online opportunities	**Online risks**
Access to global information	*Illegal content*
Educational resources	*Paedophiles, grooming, strangers*
Social networking among friends	*Extreme or sexual violence*
Entertainment, games and fun	*Other harmful offensive content*
User-generated content creation	*Racist/hate material and activities*
Civic or political participation	*Advertising and stealth marketing*
Privacy for identity expression	*Bias or misinformation*
Community involvement/activism	*Abuse of personal information*
Technological expertise and literacy	*Cyber-bullying/harassment*
Career advancement/employment	*Gambling, phishing, financial scams*
Personal/health/sexual advice	*Self-harm (suicide, anorexia)*
Specialist groups/fan forums	*Invasion/abuse of privacy*
Shared experiences with distant others	*Illegal activities (hacking, copyright abuse)*

POINTS TO CONSIDER

- *How far do you consider* commercial enterprise *to be driving internet adoption and shaping content and use?*

- *The extract claims that all previous media technological developments have raised concerns over children's exposure to harmful material – how is the internet similar/ different from these previous media forms? Are different concerns raised by this particular media development?*

- *If you look at the list of* online risks, *how far do you think these are old risks reframed for a different setting, or are they new risks altogether?*

- *Take one or two of the* online opportunities *– how would you use the internet in education to maximise the potential benefits?*

Livingstone is correct to point out the difficulty of commenting on the child's world from the perspective of an adult. There is a tendency to view one's own childhood through rose-tinted spectacles and to view social and material change with some misgiving. And this is exacerbated today by a culture in which fear is ubiquitous. Frank Furedi, who has written compellingly of a dominant *culture of fear* in modern society, recently wrote of *paranoid parenting*: where constant warnings about children's safety have left parents anxious and susceptible to scare-stories (Furedi, 2008). Stoked by media portrayals, parental anxieties cover many aspects of modern life (food safety, choking hazards, school trips, *good* parenting, public spaces....), but the internet has proved a particular focus for public panic: the fear of invisible strangers, proliferated by stories of internet grooming and paedophile rings, combined with the ease of access for children and the lack of parental control and censor.

While a distorted perception of the extent of online dangers is inevitable in such a climate, as Livingstone acknowledges, there are real threats to safety in these technologies – many of which relate directly to educational settings. Specific educational dangers include:

- false information and fraudulent sites – where pupils can access uncensored, unreviewed and unregulated material that might lack reliability, authenticity and validity;

- new forms of bullying – through online bullying via internet forums and social networking sites and posting 'happy slapping' mobile phone videos;

- homework distractions – including instant messaging, gaming, surfing, streaming and networking;

- opportunities for plagiarism – the capacity to *cut and paste* extracts from a range of electronic sources or to purchase a complete essay online;

- the emergence of a *digital divide* – where new technologies result in new inequalities, thereby creating a world of digital *haves* and *have nots*.

It is easy to become preoccupied with these dangers. But there are many potential educational benefits from emergent online and other technologies. Effective implementation opens up all sorts of learning and teaching possibilities – by promoting accessibility, communication and engagement.

143

Technology in the classroom

The schools and classrooms of the twenty-first century are very different environments to the ones that many teachers will have experienced during their own schooling. Today, children and teachers have access to a wide variety of electronic resources – both inside and outside the classroom space. There are clearly new pedagogic opportunities, especially for teachers to facilitate more *active* or *discovery* learning, and to share and make use of online resources. Technological advances offer potential to make teaching a very different sort of activity – dependent among other things on the experience, skills and values of each individual teacher, and the extent that each school embrace, support and fund technology in the classroom.

The government agency Becta (British Educational Communications and Technology Agency) was established in 1998 with the purpose of ensuring *the effective and innovative use of technology throughout learning* (www.becta.org.uk). Extract two is taken from a Becta report that reviews research on the relationship between ICT on pedagogy. The selected extract briefly outlines a number of the main findings of the report and provides a number of recommendations for the effective integration of technology into teaching. To find out more about these and other findings, you can access the full report via the organisation's website, where you can also find many publications on the relationship between technology and education.

EXTRACT TWO

Cox, M, Webb, M, Abbott, C, Blakeley, B, Beauchamp, T and Rhodes, V (2003) ICT and Pedagogy: A Review of the Literature. *Becta/DfES, pages 3–4*

Teachers' pedagogical knowledge

The teacher's own pedagogical beliefs and values play an important part in shaping technology-mediated learning opportunities. It is not yet clear from the research literature whether this results in technology being used as a 'servant' to reinforce existing teaching approaches, or as a 'partner' to change the way teacher and pupils interact with each other and with the tasks.

Teachers need extensive knowledge of ICT to be able to select the most appropriate resources. They also need to understand how to incorporate the use of ICT into their lessons; they may need to develop new pedagogies to achieve this.

Pedagogical practices of the teacher using ICT

The pedagogical practices of teachers using ICT can range from only small enhancements of practices using what are essentially traditional methods, to more fundamental changes in their approach to teaching. For example, some teachers using an interactive whiteboard have displayed content and ideas for class discussions in a traditional way, while other teachers have allowed pupils to use the whiteboard to present dramas to the whole class that they had planned and filmed themselves.

Studies show that the most effective uses of ICT are those in which the teacher and the software can challenge pupils' understanding and thinking, either through whole-class discussions using an interactive whiteboard or through individual or paired work on a computer. If the teacher has the skills to organise and stimulate the ICT-based activity, then both whole-class and individual work can be equally effective.

Organisation

The use of ICT has a limited impact on teaching and learning where teachers fail to appreciate that interactivity requires a new approach to pedagogy, lesson planning and the curriculum. Some teachers reorganise the delivery of the curriculum, but the majority use ICT to add to or enhance their existing practices. Teachers need to employ proactive and responsive strategies in order to guide, facilitate and support appropriate learning activities.

Collaborative work and insights into pupils' learning

Using ICT with pupils in pairs, groups or with a whole class, through, for example, the use of an interactive whiteboard, enables teachers to gather extensive feedback from pupils by listening to their explanations. From this, teachers are able to gain deeper insights into pupils' understanding and progress. Pupils collaborating in pairs or teams using subject-specific ICT resources are able to challenge each other's understanding and learn from such collaborations.

Effective pedagogical practices with ICT

This literature review has identified a range of practices which should be part of teachers' pedagogical frameworks if they are to integrate ICT effectively into teaching, learning and the curriculum. These include the need for teachers to:

- *understand the relationship between a range of ICT resources and the concepts, processes and skills in their subject;*

- *use their subject expertise to select appropriate ICT resources which will help them meet the specific learning objectives; this includes subject-specific software as well as more generic resources;*

- *be aware of the potential of ICT resources both in terms of their contribution to pupils' presentation skills, and their role in challenging pupils' thinking and extending their learning in a subject;*

- *develop confidence in using a range of ICT resources, via frequent practice and use beyond one or two familiar applications;*

- *appreciate that some uses of ICT will change the ways in which knowledge is represented, and the way the subject is presented to and engages pupils;*

- *know how to prepare and plan lessons where ICT is used in ways which will challenge pupils' understanding and promote greater thinking and reflection;*

- *recognise which kinds of class organisation will be most effective for particular learning tasks with ICT, for example, when pupils should work on their own, how working in pairs and groups should be organised, and when to use ICT for whole-class teaching.*

EXTRACT TWO *continued*

The majority of teachers, including the most innovative, require more knowledge of and confidence with ICT, and a better understanding of its potential to help pupils' learning. This suggests that further substantial support for continuing professional development is necessary in order that teachers integrate the use of ICT and improve pupils' attainment.

POINTS TO CONSIDER

- *What are the benefits and limitations of using technology as a pedagogic servant or a partner?*

- *Think about the use of technology on your current course of study.*

  - *How far does the technology add to your learning experience?*

  - *Are a range of interventions employed or is it one or two familiar applications?*

  - *What would make its use more effective?*

The research reviewed in extract two indicates that there is tremendous variation in the ways that ICT is understood and adopted by teachers in their professional practice. It is evident that the experiences and values of each teacher play a significant part in the ways that ICT are incorporated into their pedagogy. Lewis, focusing specifically on the internet, offers us a revealing metaphor:

Perhaps the aptest metaphor for the Internet is the jungle. The jungle provides an endless source of sustenance and delight to those who know their way in it. To those who do not, it is a dark and impenetrable maze, full of danger and unpredictable menace. In like manner, the Internet offers infinite resources to those who can navigate its limitless pathways. For those unfamiliar with it however, it can be a threatening presence, characterized by total lack of structure, full of potential predators.

(Lewis, 2004, page 3)

Rogers' model of innovation adoption (1964) is frequently used to categorise people's relationship with new technologies and with the internet in particular. Rogers, whose work predates the internet by quite some time, distinguished between *innovators*, *early* and *late adopters*, the *majority* and *laggards*: spanning those who advance and embrace innovations to those who resist and ignore them (and everyone else in between). Some teachers are happy to experiment with a range of new technologies. Many use made-for-purpose educational technologies like Blackboard or Interactive Whiteboard as a chief pedagogic tool. Others will use this type of tool, but for more marginal purposes, such as communicating lesson content or sending email. Some resist technologies in the classroom altogether, preferring learning environments more familiar to them. While many teachers use technology to facilitate more two-way communication and knowledge-sharing, others use it in ways that reinforce traditional didactic, *jug-and-mug* classroom relations.

Of course, these different relations to technology also exist in the student cohort, giving rise to a new meaning of differentiation. Teaching to the imaginary C-grade student effectively bores the A-grade student and risks overwhelming the E-grade student. Likewise, using technology in a manner appropriate to a homogenous *majority*, means stifling the creativity and independence of the technological *innovators* and alienating the *laggards* within the group.

So the increased use of ICT in the classroom gives rise to all sorts of new and complex pedagogical questions: How are teachers most effectively supported in lesson preparation and delivery? Is technology's prime purpose to enhance existing practice or to transform it? How can educational practices most effectively differentiate and accommodate different skill and experience levels? Do the adoption and use of a wide variety of ICTs by different teachers enhance or destabilise the learning experience? How far can ICTs be embedded into current practice? How can learning and teaching strategies encourage, scaffold and support laggards, while also providing freedom and stimulation for innovators?

SCENARIO

The college that Tom teaches at has implemented a peer-observation scheme. Tom is an A-level Psychology teacher, and his colleague Annie has arranged to observe his class today. The session is on the subject of the relationship between media representation and male body image. After a brief outline of the key concepts, Tom asks his class to work in pairs at computers. He gives the students 25 minutes to find evidence that they could use in a debate about the relationship between media and body image. Tom observes the students working from a distance, leaving them to work independently in pairs during the task. After 25 minutes, the students report their findings to the whole group. It is evident that a wide variety of resources have been accessed: a range of ideas and case studies are presented to the class. Tom is very pleased with how the activity worked out and he facilitates a discussion on the subject, based around the material the students have gathered. At the end of the class, Tom and Annie sit together to discuss the session. Annie enjoyed the session, but suggests that the task might have been more effective if students had been given specific tasks to do and particular websites to visit. She suggests students could have worked individually at their computer, rather than in pairs, and that each student could have been given their own question and website to access. She also expresses surprise that Tom didn't participate or help direct the students during the activity.

- *Why do you think Tom planned the session in the way he did?*

- *How might he justify to Annie the choices he made?*

- *How far do you agree with Annie's concerns and the suggestion that she makes?*

'Web 2.0' – Digital networks and the potential for new spaces for learning

In recent years, the technological advancement that has attracted most interest from academics in the field of *e-learning* or *technology enhanced practice* is Web 2.0. This centres on the capacity of the internet to provide spaces in which users are able to create, share and discuss material – which might take the form of video (most notably *YouTube*), audio (*Skype*), images (*FlickR*), text (*Twitter*) or a combination of these (*Facebook*). The key characteristic of these internet spaces is the capacity for users to communicate with one another and, in doing so, to discursively create and present new ideas and online material. Whereas previous mass media was based on one-way communication (from media outlet to audience), Web 2.0 enables multiple communication, ownership and content-generation: and it is this quality that makes Web 2.0 of particular interest to many educationalists today. In extract three, Charles Crook considers how Web 2.0 relates to the learning experience.

EXTRACT THREE

Crook, C (2008) 'What are Web 2.0 Technologies, and Why do they Matter?' in Selwyn, N, Crook, C, Noss, R and Laurillard, D (2008) Education 2.0? Designing the Web for Teaching and Learning. Technology Enhanced Learning Phase of the Teaching and Learning Research Programme. *TLRP, page 9*

Education 2.0?

Learning concepts behind web 2.0

Any educational practice that concerns the playful, expressive, reflective or exploratory aspects of knowledge building is likely to find web 2.0 tools and services a powerful resource. Moreover, educators can safely assume that most learners know about them. When directed at learning, web 2.0 impacts on four principal dimensions of the learner's experience. Two are broadly social in nature (collaboration and publication) and two are more cognitive (literacies and inquiry).

i) **Collaboration** *Web 2.0 services support communication. They allow learners to coordinate their activities to various degrees of depth. This can range from the relatively trivial level of participating in anonymous recommender systems to the more intense level of interpersonal, verbal debate. Web 2.0 may offer educators a set of tools to support forms of learning that can be more strongly collaborative and more oriented to the building of classroom communities.*

ii) **Publication** *We expect to see the work of learners on display in a classroom. The read-and-write character of web 2.0 supports users in creating original material for publication. Its relatively unbounded space can offer a strong feeling of doing authentic research when students can publish and discuss the products of their study.*

iii) **Literacies** *Culture stimulates a form of intelligence that is* literate. *Schooling cultivates a distinct orientation towards language, to which interactions with writing are crucial. Digital* *media stretch this tradition by offering new modes of representation and expression. Even the term literacy now has to be stretched to admit other forms of representational fluency than those associated with the printed word. As learners engage with digital artefacts through web 2.0, so the curriculum must address the challenge of developing their confidence with new literacies and their increased potential for creativity.*

iv) **Inquiry** *Web 2.0 technologies offer new ways for learners to conduct personal research. It creates new structures for organising data, new sources to refer to, new forms of authority, and new tools to interrogate this rich space of information. All of this has the potential to empower the student as an independent learner. But it also brings challenges to both learner and teacher. Web 2.0 knowledge structures are not navigated with the same tools or the same ease as more traditional documentary collections. It poses problems of authority and the ephemeral nature of web knowledge.*

Web 2.0 tools appear to strengthen fundamental aspects of learning that may be difficult to stimulate in learners. There are problems with web 2.0 learning in practice, but these tools do seem to mark a step change in the ways in which learners can interact with and on the web.

The report that extract 3 is from continues by focusing specifically on the feature of Web 2.0 known as *social networking*. In the final extract, Neil Selwyn considers the potential this has to enhance learning.

Selwyn, N (2008) 'Learning and Social Networking' in Selwyn, N, Crook, C, Noss, R and Laurillard, D (2008) Education 2.0? Designing the Web for Teaching and Learning. *Technology Enhanced Learning Phase of the Teaching and Learning Research Programme. TLRP, pages 18, 20*

What is social networking?

Social networking services (SNSs) are spaces for online conversations and content sharing, and are inherently capable of being personalised. A typical social networking service is based on the maintenance and sharing of users' 'profiles' – online spaces where individual users can represent themselves to other users through the display of personal information, interests, photographs, social networks and so on. Users of an SNS can maintain their own profile and access the profiles of others on the network with a view to establishing connections with preferred 'friends'.

The past five years have seen social networking become one of the most prominent and popular web 2.0 genres. Alongside the well-known MySpace and Facebook applications are more specialist social networking sites such as the business networking LinkedIn site and the Multiply site for older 'people who are settled'. Regardless of size, scope or focus, all these SNSs can be characterised as environments for democratic forms of self-expression and interaction between users. Given their broad range of features, social networking applications function in different ways depending on the preference of the user. Users can use social networking applications to 'hang out', to waste time, learn about each other or simply as a directory[1]. Learners often use social networking applications in the micro-management of their social lives, as an arena for social exploration and to develop social networking skills. The orientation of social networking applications towards self-presentation, the viewing of others' personal information and institutional life in school, university or workplace, has certainly proved attractive to younger users.

The education potential of social networking

Social networking's rise to prominence in the lives of learners has prompted enthusiasm amongst educators. Some claim that social networking applications share many of the qualities of a good 'official' education technology. They permit peer feedback and match the social contexts of learning such as the school, university or local community. The conversational, collaborative and communal qualities of social networking services are felt to "mirror much of what we know to be good models of learning, in that they are collaborative and encourage active participatory role for users"[2]. One of the main educational uses of social networking is seen to lie in their support for interaction between learners facing the common dilemma of negotiating their studies.

Social networking services may also benefit learners by allowing them to enter new networks of collaborative learning, often based on interests and affinities not catered for in their immediate educational environment. As Maloney[3] reasons, 'social networking sites such as MySpace and Facebook have shown, among other things, that students will invest time and energy in building relationships around shared interests and knowledge communities'. This has prompted some educationalists to explore the potential of social networking to augment 'conventional' interactions and dialogue between students and teachers. Some have welcomed the scope of social networking services such as Facebook to offer teachers a forum for 'easy networking and positive networking with students'[4].

But it is also apparent that some of the qualities of social networking may clash with current pedagogical paradigms. Whilst educationalists may hope that social networking promotes exchanges between learners that are related to formal educational objectives, SNSs are also celebrated for providing channels for informal and unstructured learning. It has been suggested that social networking offers the opportunity to re-engage individuals with learning and education, promoting 'critical thinking in learners' about their learning, which is one of 'the traditional objectives' of education'[5]. Some commentators say that SNSs offer "the capacity to radically change the educational system ... to better motivate students as engaged learners rather than learners who are primarily passive observers of the educational process"[6].

[1] see Stutzman, F. (2005) 'Our lives, our facebooks' www.ibibio.org/fred/pubs/stutzman_pub6.pdf

[2] see Maloney, E. (2007) 'What Web 2.0 can teach us about learning' The Chronicle of Higher Education, 53, 18, January 5th , p.B26

[3] see Maloney, E. (2007) 'What Web 2.0 can teach us about learning' The Chronicle of Higher Education, 53, 18, January 5th , p.B26

[4] see Lemeul, J. (2006) 'Why I registered on Facebook' The Chronicle of Higher Education, 53, 2, September 1st, p.C1

[5] see Bugeja, M. (2006) 'Facing the Facebook' The Chronicle of Higher Education, 52, 21, January 27th , p.C1

[6] Ziegler, S.(2007) 'The (mis)education of Generation M' Learning, Media and Technology, 32, 1, pp.69

POINTS TO CONSIDER

- *How might you guard against children posting information that:*
  - *exposes themselves to invasions of privacy and safety threats, without becoming overly censorial?;*
  - *is used for the purpose of bullying?;*
  - *purports to be the sites of teachers or head-teachers?;*
  - *gossips about and evaluates their teachers?*
- *How far can social networking tools be embedded into the curriculum and assessment?*

Increasingly, schools, colleges and universities are making use of social networking to support learning and teaching, both as part of the formal learning experience and for extended communication purposes. An example of the latter is the Parents' Schools Network. In September 2009, the government backed a new scheme to establish a social networking site for parents of secondary school pupils. Ed Balls referred to the site as a *virtual school gate*, where parents can share advice and information with each other and contact teachers. Sally Russell from Netmums claimed:

> The Parents' Schools Network has the potential to provide a virtual means of communication for parents and secondary schools...it will become a hub for every secondary school in the UK to create a dialogue between the school and parents, and also to ensure that parents themselves are engaged in providing support for each other about schooling...

(BBC, 2009)

Social networking technologies have proved to be popular with learners and teachers. In particular, they:

- stimulate conversations, democratic engagement and ownership of ideas;
- support *profound learning* (West-Burnham and Coates, 2005) through collective development of meaning and user-generated content;
- enable students to experience learning activities as authentic communal/social activities;
- make use of *digital native* skills in an authentic educational setting;
- have the capacity to make links with wider resources;
- extend *contact time* and the discursive dynamic;
- complement existing learner-centred practices.

These social networking technologies are also of particular interest to constructivist educationalists – which emphasises the active involvement of the learner in the creation of meaning. One contemporary constructivist adaptation, seeking to understand the impact and the potential of new technological learning spaces, is *communal constructivism*. From this perspective, these technologies support a learning process in which learners are actively engaged in the process of constructing knowledge for their learning community (Leask and Younie, 2001). Far from the notion of the individual learner sitting at their computer undertaking solitary tasks, communal constructivists view Web 2.0 innovations as enabling learning to become a more social activity, with online communities cultivating the shared participant experience of making and remaking meaning.

While new technologies are exciting, it is learning rather than the technology itself that must be at the heart of curriculum development and teachers' planning. And teachers must be supported in using these new technologies in ways that add real value to the overall learning environment.

C H A P T E R   S U M M A R Y

As you have seen during this chapter, the relationship between new technologies and education is complex. Clearly, as the second extract shows, there is tremendous potential for technologies to reinvigorate tired practices, to offer new ways of enhancing learning and teaching, and to provide new spaces for educational activities to take place within. But teachers need time and appropriate training to make full use of these new learning resources. As the third and fourth extracts demonstrate, Web 2.0 offers the possibility for learners to take ownership of their education. Social networking, in particular, provides learners with the chance to share their work, collaborate with one another, and participate in the construction of knowledge and communities.

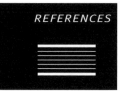
REFERENCES

BBC (2009) 'Parents get 'virtual school gate' **http://news.bbc.co.uk/1/hi/education/8268528.stm**

Furedi, F (2008) *Paranoid parenting (2nd edition).* London: Continuum Press

Leask, M, and Younie, S (2001) 'Communal constructivist theory: pedagogy of information and communications technology & internationalisation of the curriculum', *Journal of Information Technology for Teacher Education,* Vol. 10, Nos 1 & 2, pages 117–134

Lewis, G (2004) *The internet and young learners.* Resource books for teachers (Series Editor Maley, A) Oxford: Oxford University Press

Prensky, M (2001) 'Digital natives, digital immigrants'. *On the Horizon, 9 (5),* October 2001

Rogers, E (1964) *Diffusion of Innovations.* Glencoe: Free Press

West-Burnham, J and Coates, M (2005) *Personalizing Learning: Transforming education for every child.* Continuum

FURTHER READING

Beetham, H and Sharpe , R (Eds) (2007) *Rethinking pedagogy for a digital age: Designing and delivering e-learning.* Abingdon: Routledge

Holmes, B and Gardner, J (2006) *E-learning: concepts and practices* London: Sage Publications

Lewis, L and Allan, B (2005) *Virtual learning communities: A guide for practitioners.* Maidenhead: Open University Press

Marsh, J (2006) *Popular culture, new media and digital literacy in early childhood.* London: Routledge

Selwyn, N and Facier, K (2007) *Opening education beyond the digital divide: Rethinking digital inclusion for the 21st century.* Bristol: Futurelab

WEBSITES

www.becta.org.uk/

www.free-ed.net/

www.worldinternetproject.net/

www.teachers.tv/

http://schoolofeverything.com/

Chapter 11

Education beyond formal schooling

OBJECTIVES

By the end of this chapter you should have:
- identified a variety of forms, distinguishing characteristics and purposes of informal education;
- reflected on the similarities and differences between formal and informal education;
- considered ways of promoting and organising learning outside formal schooling;
- understood the significance of networks for learning outside formal education;
- examined how socio-technical developments in the twenty-first century compel us to rethink educational structures.

Introduction

When we think about education, we tend to think of it in its formal sense – the types of activities that take place in specific buildings or institutions (schools, colleges and universities), at particular times of our lives (from the ages of 5 to 16, 18, or 21) and involving distinctive groups of participants – teachers doing the *educating* and pupils or students being *educated*. But this 'formal' sense of education is relatively new, especially as something that continues beyond childhood and that includes more or less every member of society. Until very recently, for instance, a higher education was the preserve of a small elite – many of you will be the first generation in your family to study at university.

In fact, the majority of the things we learn through our lives, we learn outside of these formal settings: from our parents, siblings and friends, from newspapers, books, television and internet, in our places of work, as members of the various communities we belong to, during the conversations we have. Instead of the conventional classroom, we learn in community centres, after school and youth clubs, museums, libraries, cafes, or at home. This chapter introduces the notion of 'informal education', examining what makes it distinct from more formal forms. It considers how education might be organised around less formal structures and reflects on how changes in wider society and developments in technology mean a greater role for education outside the traditional school setting in future years.

Informal education

Informal learning activities considerably predate the *formal* institutions that typify education today. We were engaged in the processes of learning and teaching well before any schools, colleges or universities came into existence. On the infed.org website from which the following extract is taken, Smith identifies *informal education* activities back through time and across the planet (Smith, 1997). He traces *specialist educators* and *non-formal* educational settings to ancient Greece 2,500 years ago and argues that the values and practices that underpin informal education today owe much to the dialogues and debates characteristic of that time (Jeffs and Smith, 2005, page 10).

In the opening section of the first extract, Smith identifies three types of activity that might be described as informal education:

- the unintentional or inadvertent learning that takes place through our *everyday* experience;

- the learning tasks we might plan and initiate for ourselves;

- the learning we undertake as a member of an organisation, like a community group or a youth club.

Many view the third of these as a different sort of activity to the first two. Whereas the first two generally don't depend on the involvement of an *educator*, the third one does. The third activity seems to have more in common with formal education – a particular time and place for the learning activity to occur, defined roles of learners and teachers, and relatively explicit learning outcomes. As a result, many make a three-way distinction – between *formal education* (schools and colleges), *informal education* (at home, with parents and friends) and *non-formal education* (organised learning outside of formal systems) (see La Belle, 1984). Smith, on the other hand, views substantial overlap and similarity in terms of aim and process between the informal and non-formal – as is evident in the following extract.

EXTRACT ONE

Smith, M (1997) 'Introducing Informal Education: What is Informal Education? Where does it Happen? How has it Developed?' Informal Education *website – www.infed.org/hp-intro.htm*

Some see informal education as the learning that goes on in daily life. As friends, for example, we may well encourage others to talk about things that have happened in their lives so that they can handle their feelings and to think about what to do next. As parents or carers we may show children how to write different words or tie their laces. As situations arise we respond.

Others may view informal education as the learning projects that we undertake for ourselves. We may take up quilting, for example, and then start reading around the subject, buying magazines and searching out other quilters (perhaps through joining a Quilters Guild).

Many view informal education as the learning that comes as part of being involved in youth and community organizations. In these settings there are specialist workers / educators whose job it is to encourage people to think about experiences and situations. Like friends or parents they may respond to what is going on but, as professionals, these workers are able to bring special insights and ways of working.

Informal education can be all of these things. It is a process – a way of helping people to learn.

So what is informal education?

In the examples above we can see that whether we are parents or specialist educators, we teach. When we are engaged in learning projects we teach ourselves. In all of these roles we are also likely to talk and join in activities with others (children, young people and adults). Some of the time we work with a clear objective in mind – perhaps linked to some broader plan e.g. around the development of reading. At other times we may go with the flow – adding to the conversation when it seems right or picking up on an interest.

These ways of working all entail learning – but informal education tends to be unpredictable – we do not know where it might lead. In conversation we have to catch the moment where we can say or do something to deepen people's thinking or to put themselves in touch with their feelings.

'Going with the flow' opens up all sorts of possibilities for us as educators. On one hand we may not be prepared for what comes, on the other we may get into rewarding areas. There is the chance, for example, to connect with the questions, issues and feelings that are important to people, rather than what we think might be significant.

Picking our moment in the flow is also likely to take us into the world of people's feelings, experiences and relationships. While all educators should attend to experience and encourage people to reflect, informal educators are thrown into this. For the most part, we do not have lesson plans to follow; we respond to situations, to experiences.

Such conversations and activities can take place anywhere. This contrasts with formal education which tends to take place in special settings such as schools. However, we should not get too tied up with the physical setting for the work. Formal education can also take place in almost any other location – such as teaching someone to add up while shopping in the market. Here it is the special sort of social setting we have to create that is important. We build an atmosphere or grab an opportunity, so that we may teach.

Obviously, informal educators work informally – but we also do more formal things. We spend time with people in everyday settings – but we also create opportunities for people to study experiences and questions in a more focused way. This could mean picking up on something that is said in a conversation and inviting those involved to take it further. For example, we may be drinking tea with a couple of women in a family or health centre who are asking questions about cervical cancer. We may suggest they look at some materials that we have and talk about they see. Alternatively, it could mean we set up a special session, or organize a course. We may also do some individual tutoring, for example, around reading and writing. Just as school teachers may work informally for part of their time, so informal educators may run classes or teach subjects. The difference between them lies in the emphasis they put on each.

So what is informal education? From what we have looked at so far we can say the following. Informal education:

- *works through, and is driven by, conversation.*

- *involves exploring and enlarging experience.*

- *can take place in any setting.*

However, there is more – purpose.

... and the purpose of informal education?
At one level, the purpose of informal education is no different to any other form of education. In one situation we may focus on, say, healthy eating, in another family relationships. However, running through all this is a concern to build the sorts of communities and relationships in which people can be happy and fulfilled. John Dewey once described this as educating so that people may share in a common life. Those working as informal educators have a special contribution to make here.

A focus on conversation is central to building communities. The sorts of values and behaviours needed for conversation to take place are exactly what are required if neighbourliness and democracy are to flourish. What is more, the sorts of groups informal educators such as youth and social action workers work with – voluntary, community-based, and often concerned with mutual aid – are the bedrock of democratic societies.

It comes as no surprise then, that those working as informal educators tend to emphasize certain values. These include commitments to:

- *work for the well-being of all.*

- *respect the unique value and dignity of each human being.*

- *dialogue.*

- *equality and justice.*

- *democracy and the active involvement of people in the issues that affect their lives.*

As informal educators we have to spend a lot of time thinking about the values that run through our work. We do not have a curriculum or guiding plan for a lot of the work, so we have to consider how we should respond to situations. This involves going back to core values. Reflecting on these allows us to make judgements about what might best help people to share in a common life.

Why have specialist informal educators, what sets them apart?

As we have seen, everyone is an educator – but some people are recognized or appointed to teach and to foster learning. There are three main reasons why specialist informal educators may be needed. First, it may be that some situations demand a deeper under-standing or wider range of skills than many of us develop in our day to day lives. Through reflection and training specialists can become sophisticated facilitators of groups and of conversations with individuals. They can also develop a certain wisdom about people and situations because of the opportunities they have. In many communities the role may be fulfilled and developed by 'elders' or by those who are recognized to be wise. In other situations, often linked to the development of capitalism, there has been an increased division of labour. Additional or alternative forms of learning and teaching are needed.

Second, it may be that people do not have the time to spend exchanging and learning with others in the ways they wish or need. Because of their situation, they may not have a chance to engage in the sorts of conversations they find fulfilling. Where we, for example, have to work some distance from home, deal with complex systems or have so much to do simply to get by, the amount of time we can spend in open talk can shrink. In addi-tion, we may choose not to spend time in conversation or doing things with others. With our increased use of different (and often individualized) entertainment media such as tel-evision, the amount of time we spend directly engaging with others may well be lessened.

Third, a good deal of the work that informal educators engage in is with other profes-sionals. For example, an informal educator working in a school will have to spend a lot of their time deepening and extending the understanding and orientation of teachers and other staff. With the pressure to produce results and to achieve good test scores, relation-ships and processes can be easily neglected. Furthermore, there can be a narrowing of educational focus. In these situations, while informal educators may be appointed to work with students, they have to encourage and educate staff so that the needs of students can be recognized and, hopefully, met. To do this informal educators will often need both to develop a detailed understanding of the situation, and (in that status-conscious world) have some sort of professional qualification.

So what sets informal educators apart? If we examine what they are doing, a number of characteristics emerge. They:

- *place conversation at the centre of their activities.*

- *operate in a wide range of settings – often within the same day. These include centres, schools and colleges, streets and shopping malls, people's homes, workplaces, and social, cultural and sporting settings.*

- *look to explore and enlarge experience.*

- *put a special emphasis on building just and democratic relationships and organizations.*

- *use a variety of methods including groupwork, casual conversation, play, activities, work with individuals and casework. While their work for much of the time is informal – they also make use of more formal approaches to facilitate learning.*

EXTRACT ONE *continued*

- *work with people of all ages although many will specialize around a special age range e.g. children, young people or with adults. In other words informal education is life-long education.*

- *develop particular special interests such as in children's play and development; community development and community action; literacy and basic education; advice; outdoor and adventure activities; arts and cultural work; and youth work.*

POINTS TO CONSIDER

- *Find a couple of instances of informal education in your local area – you may or may not take part in them yourself. How closely does Smith's account (a focus on feelings, well-being, experience, conversation, active involvement, going-with-the-flow, equality, democratic relations, community...) correspond with your own examples?*

- *Think about the similarities and differences between formal and informal education and between the qualified teacher and the specialist informal educator – are many/any of the characteristics of the informal educator (as identified by Smith) also applicable to formal educators?*

The current policy-driven emphasis on *lifelong learning* and *widening participation* appears to blur the boundaries between informal education, as outlined in the extract, and more formal institutions. Over the last 15 years or so, schools, colleges and universities have been encouraged (and funded) to reach out to non-traditional learners and to non-traditional settings. There has been a rapid expansion in the numbers of learners in both further and higher education and an extension of work-based learning through schemes such as Train to Gain. There are far greater opportunities to engage in flexible, online and distance learning. Initiatives like Playing for Success have sought to provide less formal learning environments for school-age learners and Sure Start has extended learning into the heart of the community. Adult learners have returned to study in a wide range of areas and levels: from literacy, numeracy and IT basic skills courses, to GCSE, A-level, Access and degrees programmes of study. In 2009, around 39 per cent of the adult population were participating in learning, with more than 3 million in further education and nearly 350,000 in higher education (NIACE, 2009, page 2).

Yet, in 2009, a major report into the future of lifelong learning questioned the extent that formal schooling appropriately prepares school-leavers for a life of learning. Claxton and Lucas talk of the need for a *re-imagining of schools as apprenticeships in the craft and the pleasure of lifelong learning* (Claxton and Lucas, 2009, page 25). While they celebrate recent initiatives like the RSAs Opening Minds competence-led curriculum, they argue that a widespread emphasis on exam results and other performance indicators results in a restrictive, assessment-focused curriculum that does little to foster lifelong learning qualities.

A 'deschooled' society?

So why might the existence of *formal* educational institutions and *expert* teachers have a harmful impact on learning? It might encourage an assumption that learning takes place in special buildings, at specific times of our lives, in the hands of trained and qualified professionals (and, correspondingly, not in other places, at other times, with other people). It might make us think that when we have completed schooling, we have finished the part of our life when we are supposed to learn. Indeed, we may have had a fairly unpleasant experience of our own schooling, perhaps failing courses, struggling with difficult material or being bullied, and this might result in us being turned off learning for good. It might be, most damningly, that the kinds of skills and attitudes we glean from our experiences in formal education inhibit our capacity for independent autonomous learning as we get older.

This is a viewpoint associated with 'deschoolers' who argue that institutional formal education is harmful to individuals and to societies. By imposing a one-size-fits-all version of education, it diverts us from learning what we want, where and how we want, at our own self-determined pace. Most problematically, the institutionalisation of learning persuades us to perceive education as a product to be consumed, rather than an activity. It becomes something that we acquire from a service provider – who, by virtue of the monopoly they possess, is able to define, restrict and control it. Education becomes commodified – we say *I've got an education* (meaning we have acquired a number of certificates) or, even worse, we say, *I've got a public school education* (meaning we have paid money to gain a supposed premium service).

Ivan Illich, one of the most influential of theorists to adopt this *deschooling* position, offers us a radically different vision for education. In the *deschooled society* he envisages, learning is organised in terms of informal, voluntary and widespread networks or *learning webs*.

EXTRACT TWO

Illich, I (1971) Deschooling Society. *Harmondsworth: Penguin Books, pages 77–79*

Four networks

The planning of new educational institutions ought not to begin with the administrative goals of a principal or president, or with the teaching goals of a professional educator, or with the learning goals of any hypothetical class of people. It must not start with the question, 'What should someone learn?' but with the question, 'What kinds of things and people might learners want to be in contact with in order to learn?'

Someone who wants to learn knows that he needs both information and critical response to its use from somebody else. Information can be stored in things and in persons. In a good educational system access to things ought to be available at the sole bidding of the learner, while access to informants requires, in addition, others' consent. Criticism can also come from two directions: from peers or from elders, that is, from fellow learners whose immediate interests match mine, or from those who will grant me a share in their

---

superior experience. Peers can be colleagues with whom to raise a question, companions for playful and enjoyable (or arduous) reading or walking, challengers at any type of game. Elders can be consultants on which skill to learn, which method to use, what company to seek at a given moment. They can be guides to the right questions to be raised among peers and to the deficiency of the answers they arrive at. Most of these resources are plentiful. But they are neither conventionally perceived as educational resources, nor is access to them for learning purposes easy, especially for the poor. We must conceive of new relational structures which are deliberately set up to facilitate access to these resources for the use of anybody who is motivated to seek them for his education. Administrative, technological, and especially legal arrangements are required to set up such web-like structures.

Educational resources are usually labeled according to educators' curricular goals. I propose to do the contrary, to label four different approaches which enable the student to gain access to any educational resource which may help him to define and achieve his own goals:

1. *Reference Services to Educational Objects – which facilitate access to things or processes used for formal learning. Some of these things can be reserved for this purpose, stored in libraries, rental agencies, laboratories, and showrooms like museums and theaters; others can be in daily use in factories, airports, or on farms, but made available to students as apprentices or on off hours.*

2. *Skill Exchanges – which permit persons to list their skills, the conditions under which they are willing to serve as models for others who want to learn these skills, and the addresses at which they can be reached.*

3. *Peer-Matching – a communications network which permits persons to describe the learning activity in which they wish to engage, in the hope of finding a partner for the inquiry.*

4. *Reference Services to Educators-at-Large – who can be listed in a directory giving the addresses and self-descriptions of professionals, paraprofessionals, and free-lancers, along with conditions of access to their services. Such educators, as we will see, could be chosen by polling or consulting their former clients.*

POINTS TO CONSIDER

Try to come up with your own contemporary examples of:

- *reference services to educational objects;*

- *skill exchanges;*

- *peer matching;*

- *references services to educators-at-large.*

What do you see as the main advantages and disadvantages of Illich's more informal, voluntaristic and widespread educational arrangements?

How might the social, cultural and technological composition of the twenty-first century fit more appropriately with the learning networks or webs that Illich articulates in the extract?

SCENARIO

Consider the following example of a skill exchange based on social networking – the School of Everything. You were introduced to social networking in an earlier chapter – the School of Everything is one of the examples the reading goes on to outline:

> *The School of Everything is a social networking service that seeks to connect individuals with an interest in learning with individuals who are willing and able to teach. As the site's motto puts it,* Everyone has something to learn, everyone has something to teach. *Members of the School of Everything community are encouraged to maintain profiles which describe what they are willing to teach and where. They might be professional tutors or interested amateurs. Potential learners can search through the community to find the teaching provision that best fits their needs and location. Although some commentators have styled the* School of Everything *as an eBay for stuff that does not get taught in school[7], the service is not primarily focused on for-profit tuition. The site is free to use, and interested teachers are encouraged to offer their services for free or else negotiate fees with the community. It is intended to stimulate a 'bottom-up' supply of teaching in contrast to the 'top-down' supply of instruction through the formal education system.*

> *(Selwyn, 2008, page 20)*

[7] see Leadbetter, C. (2008) 'People power transforms the web in next online revolution' The Observer, March 9th, p.26

The example of the School of Everything in the scenario above provides an indication of how Illich's vision might be realised in the twenty-first century. Since Illich was writing, people have become far more mobile, there has been a huge expansion in the leisure, media and consumer industries, and information and communication technologies can put us in touch with a far wider variety of ideas and people. Spend a brief time on the internet and you will find masses of people offering and seeking learning experiences. For instance,

Illich would have celebrated the increased accessibility of information – enabling you to research healthy lifestyles or possible causes and treatments for symptoms independently. This gives you more power over your own health, it means you do not need to be reliant on the *medical expertise* and it can rebalance the power-relations when you do visit your GP (of course, it can also be a source of additional worry for the hypochondriac!).

Although it is difficult to imagine the kinds of educational structures Illich articulates replacing existing formal schooling structures, it seems plausible that they will have a prominent role in the twenty-first century. Illich contends that learning encounters ought to be voluntarily instigated by the learner, not by the professional educator making decisions about what ought and ought not be learnt – and this seems more appropriate to a modern world that places high value on individual sovereignty. An effective *bottom-up* or *demand-side* model requires educational networks that are accessible and extensive. While there would clearly be concerns over safety and the quality of the provision on offer, learners would benefit greatly from having the choice about what, where, when and how they learn, as well as who they learn with and who or what they learn from. Arguably a true *learning society* cannot be achieved by broadening the scope of formal schooling, but by cultivating the kinds of *learning webs* or networks that Illich outlines.

A networked education for the twenty-first century

According to the influential social theorist Manuel Castells and others, the defining characteristic of the modern era is the emergence of networks. Since the latter part of the twentieth century, social structures and activities have become organised around information networks: we live within an electronically interconnected system of information and people (Castells, 2000). Developments in technology enable the organisation of information, production, consumption, communication and power outside the confines of location, in globalised, decentralised, flexible and (increasingly) open networks.

The third extract is taken from a report of Futurelab's Beyond Current Horizons programme: exploring social and technological change and the potential challenges and opportunities these mean for education. The report identifies a number of likely socio-technical developments in the next few decades, including:

- more information stored and accessed about more aspects of life;

- individuals in *perpetual contact* with networks and communities;

- machines taking on more roles traditionally undertaken by humans;

- growing sense of *together apart* – as work, family, leisure interactions are not limited to geographical location;

- *weakening of institutional boundaries* – for example, between workplace and home, work and retirement, public and private;

- a widening of inequality. (Facer, 2009, pages 3–5)

Facer, K (2009) 'Educational, Social and Technological Futures: a Report from the Beyond Current Horizons Programme'. Beyond Current Horizons: Technology, Children, Schools and Families. Bristol: Futurelab, pages 6–8

What are the key challenges for education posed by these potential socio-technical changes?

At the heart of educational processes is a concern with enabling individuals to learn to build, share, manipulate, communicate and generate knowledge. The developments described above suggest that we need to pay increasing attention to the role of socio-technical networks in these knowledge processes over the coming two decades. These developments suggest that:

- *We need to assume that individuals will be constantly networked to people, tools and resources*

- *Network technologies will amplify and intensify the existing role of social networks in shaping access to, and production of, knowledge*

- *Existing inequalities will continue to be played out through socio-technical networks*

The socio-technical developments described above also suggest that the coming two decades may see a significant shift away from the equation of 'learning' with 'educational institutions' that emerged with industrialisation, toward a more mixed, diverse and complex learning landscape which sees formal and informal learning taking place across a wide range of different sites and institutions. These developments suggest that:

- *New providers from private, public and third sector organisations in the UK and internationally will offer widely accessible face to face, remote, work-based and informal education*

- *Distinctions between sites of education, leisure and work and between stages of education, working, caring and retirement will erode*

- *Informal learning, including inter-generational learning, will play an increasingly important role in social cohesion and educational provision*

Since the early 1990s, the idea of the 'knowledge economy' has shaped education policy in the UK and around the world. This idea has led to a commitment to widening university participation, raising the school leaving age, increased investment in creative practice and STEM subjects, and the demand for a universal rise in formal qualifications and accreditation of skills. The 'knowledge economy' is, itself, dependent upon a particular interpretation of socio-technical developments: it assumes that there will be increased economic competition between countries, facilitated by global information and communications infrastructures; and that this competition can be managed in the UK by ensuring that citizens are sufficiently skilled to take on high-value, creative and knowledge-generating employment while low paid jobs are offshored to other countries who compete on price.

The socio-technical developments described above, however, suggest that this vision of a thriving and universally beneficial UK knowledge economy focused on creative industries, knowledge work and innovation, may be increasingly hard to sustain over the coming two decades; and that its benefits are not necessarily likely to accrue to all citizens in the form of fulfilling, well rewarded employment. These developments suggest that:

- *We may see an increasing polarisation in the labour market between highly paid global knowledge workers and low skilled, low paid service workers*

- *One response to this polarisation may be a shift in social and cultural values towards a valuing of ordinary work, and a recognition of informal and community economies*

- *Another response to this polarisation may be a shift toward new sites of economic activity and increased emphasis on locally focused entrepreneurialism*

How might education systems need to change in the light of socio-technical developments?

These developments pose three key challenges for educators and education systems wishing to enable learners to flourish in the coming two decades:

They require us to redesign educational practices to meet the needs of networked individuals

They require us to develop systemic strategies to support learners to navigate a much more complex learning landscape

They require us to re-examine our educational goals in the context of economic uncertainties.

In respect of current formal educational provision, this implies the following aspirations:

1 *The design of a 'curriculum for networked learning'*

- *This should comprise, for example, opportunities for learners to learn and work within meaningful socio-technical networks not wholly within single educational institutions; to be assessed in interaction with tools, resources and collaborators; to develop capacities to manage information and intellectual property, build reputation and trust, develop experience of working remotely and in mediated environments; to create new learning networks; to reflect upon how learning is connected with other areas of personal, social, and working lives and manage and negotiate these relationships; to explore the human-machine relationships involved in socio-technical networks.*

2 *The creation of open, flexible and networked relationships across diverse educational institutions, both formal and informal*

- *This would include, for example, compatible personal learning records owned and managed by learners that can be carried across diverse settings; interoperable systems and standards that enable learners to demonstrate attainment and experience across diverse settings; timetabling arrangements and tools that enable learners flexibly to build timetables across different providers to take advantage of learning opportunities in schools, museums, community settings, workplaces, universities, and homes; a map of the diverse learning landscape that can support learners and mentors to navigate this complex environment effectively.*

3 *The development of a mentoring and networking workforce*

- *This would include: a cohort of lifelong mentors or guides to ensure learners can take informed choices from diverse education providers and balance education, working, caring and personal development choices across the lifecourse and at key transitions; the diversification of teacher 'identities' to include experts in workplaces, community educators, school and university lecturers, and voluntary providers; a review of existing child protection and CRB arrangements; a cohort of educators skilled in establishing and working within social networks across institutions and ages.*

4 *The provision of intelligent information and improved forums for public debate on the educational implications of socio-technical change*

- *This would include: widely accessible and rigorous information on the field of brain science, genetics and computer science in education; and public forums for educators, parents, children, industry and community to debate and design educational responses to the ethical questions raised by, for example, changed human-machine relationships or the role of global education providers in the education arena.*

POINTS TO CONSIDER

- *What do you understand by a curriculum for networked learning? What do you see as the main differences with the National Curriculum today?*

- *How similar/different are the proposals in this extract from the* learning webs *that Illich articulated in the previous extract?*

- *Do you agree that socio-technological developments are, and will continue to have the effect of, polarising existing inequalities? Is there any alternative?*

- *How do you feel about the notion of a* mixed, diverse and complex learning landscape?

As the twenty-first century progresses, the idea that learning is something that takes place solely in formal educational settings seems increasingly at odds with lived experiences. Our modern way of life is increasingly mobile, complex and fluid. Correspondingly, we search for, and require, varied learning experiences at different times, places and stages of life. Formal schooling environments remain central to learning, but not the exclusive domain that they have been seen as in the past. Rather, in the *network society*, schools, colleges and universities need to become, what Leadbeater terms, *hubs of learning* (2000, page 227), capable of reaching out into communities and drawing in various skills and experiences. As centres of learning networks, these institutions can cultivate the skills and attitudes that make us capable of traversing a new and exciting learning landscape.

C H A P T E R   S U M M A R Y

This chapter has outlined some of the main similarities and differences between formal and informal education. It has examined the capacity for networks (both face-to-face and online) to offer alternative possibilities for learning. Finally, it has considered how social and technological developments in the first half of the twenty-first century provide new challenges and opportunities for learning. As networks become increasingly significant in our daily lives, they are likely to open up all sorts of fresh learning opportunities.

Castells, M (2000) *The rise of the network society, the information age: economy, society and culture* Vol. I. (2nd edition). Oxford: Blackwell

Claxton, G and Lucas, B (2009) 'Schools as a foundation for lifelong learning: The implications of a lifelong learning perspective for the re-imagining of school-age education'. *Inquiry into the future for lifelong learning: sector paper 1*. National Institute of Adult Continuing Education (NIACE)

Jeffs, T and Smith, M (2005) *Informal education (3rd edition)*. Nottingham: Educational Heretics Press

La Belle, T (1984) 'Formal, non-formal and informal education: a holistic perspective on lifelong learning'. *International Review of Education*, 28 (2), June 1982 pp. 159–175

Leadbeater, C (2000) *Living on thin air: the new economy*. Harmondsworth: Penguin Books

NIACE (2009) *Making a difference for adult learners: NIACE policy impact report 2009*. National Institute of Adult Continuing Education

Selwyn, N (2008) 'Learning and social networking'. In Noss, R. (ed.) Education 2.0? *Designing the web for teaching and learning*. TRLP

Smith, M (1997) 'A brief history of thinking about informal education' *Informal Education website –* **www.infed.org/thinkers/et-hist.htm**

Bentley, T (ed.) (1998) *Learning beyond the classroom*. London: Routledge

Deer Richardson, L and Wolfe, M (ed.) (2001) *Principles and practice of informal education: learning through life*. London: Routledge

Jeffs, T and Smith, M (2005) *Informal education (3rd edition)*. Nottingham: Educational Heretics Press

www.lifelonglearning.co.uk

www.lotc.org.uk/ – Learning Outside the Classroom

www.u3a.org.uk/ – University of the Third Age

Index